OCS Study
MMS 2004-013

Intermediate Depth Circulation in the Gulf of Mexico: PALACE Float Results for the Gulf of Mexico Between April 1998 and March 2002

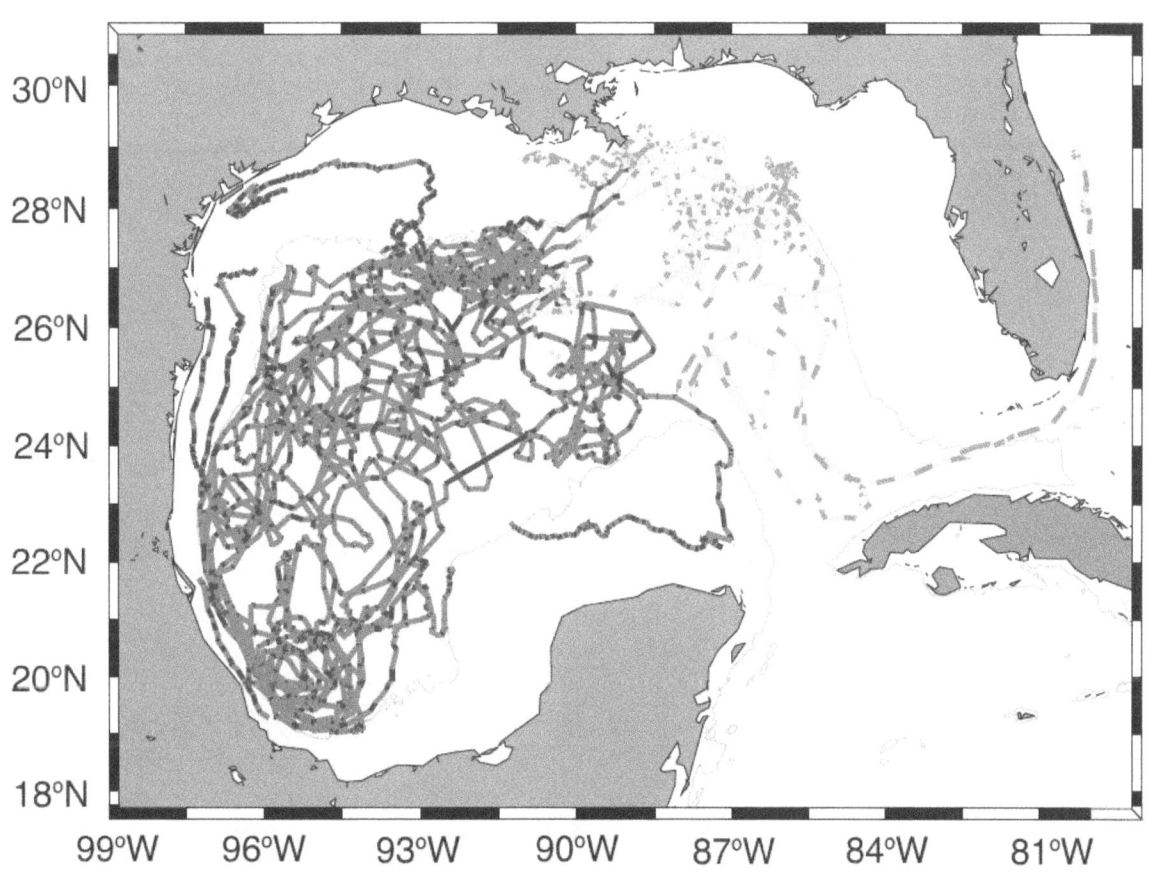

U.S. Department of the Interior
Minerals Management Service
Gulf of Mexico OCS Region

OCS Study
MMS 2004-013

Intermediate Depth Circulation in the Gulf of Mexico: PALACE Float Results for the Gulf of Mexico Between April 1998 and March 2002

Author and Principal Investigator

George L. Weatherly

Prepared under MMS Contract
1435-01-00-CT-31105
by
Florida State University
Department of Oceanography
Tallahassee, FL 32306-4320

Published by

U.S. Department of the Interior
Minerals Management Service
Gulf of Mexico OCS Region

New Orleans
March 2004

DISCLAIMER

This report was prepared under a contract from the Minerals Management Service (MMS) to the Florida State University. This report has been technically reviewed by the MMS and approved for publication. Approval does not signify that the contents necessarily reflect the views and policies of the Service, nor does mention of trade names or commercial products constitute endorsement or recommendation for use. It is, however, exempt from review and compliance with the MMS editorial standards.

REPORT AVAILABILITY

Extra copies of the report may be obtained from the Publication Information Office (Mail Stop 5034) at the following address:

U. S. Department of the Interior
Minerals Management Service
Gulf of Mexico OCS Region
Public Information Office (MS 5034)
1201 Elmwood Park Blvd.
New Orleans, LA 70123-2394

Telephone Number: 1-800-200-GULF
or 504-736-2519

CITATION

Suggested citation:

Weatherly, G. Intermediate Depth Circulation in the Gulf of Mexico: PALACE Float Results for the Gulf of Mexico Between April 1998 and March 2002. U.S. Dept. of the Interior, Minerals Management Service, Gulf of Mexico OCS Region, New Orleans, LA. OCS Study MMS 2004-013. 51 pp.

ABOUT THE COVER

This map of the Gulf of Mexico shows all the subsurface (red or green) and surface (blue or yellow) PALACE float trajectories. The floats were launched in the northern Gulf of Mexico and dispersed throughout the Gulf. However, those floats launched in the eastern Gulf (yellow green) tended to stay there and those launched in the western Gulf (red blue) tended to stay there. The 900-m isobath is shown.

ACKNOWLEDGMENTS

This study analyzes PALACE float data obtained in the Gulf of Mexico by others. We gratefully acknowledge MMS for the support and the foresight to analyze this unique data set. Dr. Carole Current, the Contracting Officer's Technical Representative, has been most supportive in the technical aspects of this project. We benefited from Dr. Alexis Lugo-Fernandez' knowledge of the Gulf of Mexico. We are grateful to them for the manner in which they encouraged the work reported here.

Daniel Webb of Webb Research, Falmouth, Massachusetts, archived the raw data, made it available us and helped us to decipher it. He also maintained a web site showing results of preliminary processing done at Webb Research which we found very useful. When this web site was shut down he passed the information on it to us, and in turn we have put it on our web sites which are referenced in this report. We are very grateful to him for his assistance. We are grateful to Robert Leben for providing us with satellite altimeter maps.

Dr. Nicolas Wienders did much of the analysis reported here and for which we are very grateful. He built upon the work done earlier by Dr. Anastasia Romanou who worked with Georges Weatherly when an earlier phase of the PALACE float analysis was funded by the National Oceanographic Partners Program. We are grateful for Romanou's help in learning and building from her experiences.

Reinard Harkema, the data analysis person of the Current Meter Facility at Florida State University, assisted in all phases of the data analysis. Paula Tamaddoni Jahromi also actively participated in the analysis as well as the administrative oversight. They were both invaluable in this study.

TABLE OF CONTENTS

LIST OF FIGURES

vi

LIST OF FIGURES

(continued)

LIST OF TABLES

1.0 EXECUTIVE SUMMARY

Seventeen PALACE floats were set in the Gulf of Mexico in 1998 as part of a study of the Gulf of Mexico by the National Oceanographic Partners Program (NOPP). The Principal Investigator (PI) was asked to examine data after the floats were deployed. When funding for the NOPP program was not renewed the PI successfully asked MMS for support to complete the analysis of the float data. This is a report of that analysis.

This is a report of the first ever study of the intermediate depth circulation in the Gulf of Mexico made using free-drifting floats. The floats were fitted with temperature sensors, and this study also reports the first ever study of the intermediate depth thermal structure of the Gulf made by profiling floats. The floats were set in the northern Gulf of Mexico but quickly dispersed resulting in observations being made throughout the Gulf of Mexico.

The floats drifted at ≈900-m depth coming up to the surface once a week for 12 hours to be positioned by satellite and to download their temperature profile data. Only the results of their drift at ≈900-m depth are reported here. It is important to note that if the drift of the floats while they were at the surface and transiting to and from the surface had not been eliminated as done here a very different view of the intermediate depth circulation would have emerged. The surface drift was often comparable to or greater than that at depth and not always in the same direction.

About 30% of the Gulf of Mexico is continental shelf, and groundings on the shelf were a major problem. When the floats were up at the surface once a week it was not unusual for them to drift onto the continental shelf and consequently sink to the bottom on their next dive. Only about 50% of the profiles which could have been made were made in water of depth >900 m, the floats drift depth.

The float deep drifts, obtained in the period April 1998 - March 2003, indicate that 900-m depth is not a level of no motion in the Gulf of Mexico. One major result of the study is that there appears to be cyclonic flow along the border of and through out the Gulf of Mexico, and that this flow intensifies into a ≈10 cm/s southward flowing current in the western Bay of Campeche. An unexpected result was that there was a strong tendency for floats launched in the eastern Gulf to remain there and for floats launched in the western Gulf to remain there.

The floats indicated both in their deep drifts and in their temperature profiles that the Loop Current and Loop Current Rings extend down to at least ≈900-m depth. The current at ≈900-m depth beneath these features was about 20% that at the surface, but the direction of flow at depth relative to that at the surface appeared to have no clear pattern.

Subsurface cold, cyclonic eddies extending downward from ≈300-m depth down to at least ≈900-m depth were seen both in the deep drifts and in the temperature profiles. These ≈100-km diameter features were not evident in satellite altimeter maps and tended to move westward at ≈3-5 cm/s and have orbital velocities at ≈900-m depth of ≈10-15 cm/s. The temperature data obtained indicate that these subsurface cold eddies may be formed from cold core rings originally having a surface expression.

The 1,481 temperature profiles obtained in the open Gulf in water of depths >200 m indicated that the presence of coastal riverine water throughout the open Gulf of Mexico is common.

1

About half of the profiles showed such evidence. Their presence was relatively rare in the summer and more common in the winter, and this seems consistent with results seen in LATEX drifters.

The temperature profiles also revealed that surface mixed layers could be rather thick ($\approx$50 m to $\approx$170 m) in the open Gulf in the winter. These thicker layers were generally seen in the Loop Current and Loop Current Rings which implies considerable heat loss in the winter in these features.

The greatest temperature variability of 14°C was found at $\approx$150-m depth and exceeded that seen in the surface layer. The greatest vertical excursion of isotherms was for the colder ones around 7°C where it approached 600 m. The vertical displacement of isotherms by the presence of the Loop Current, Loop Current and cold core rings resulted in greater thermal variability in the thermocline than in the seasonally modulated surface layer.

When grounded the PALACE floats yielded temperature profiles which differ from those usually obtained with CTDs in that they go to the bottom while the latter usually are terminated $\approx$10 m above the bottom. Temperature profiles obtained from grounded floats often showed anomalously cold bottom mixed layers of thickness $\approx$20 m.

2.0 INTRODUCTION

This report presents the results of 17 satellite-tracked deep floats set in the Northern Gulf of Mexico. The floats were acquired and set by Dr. John Blaha of NAVOCEANO in 1988 as part of a NOPP (National Oceanographic Partners Program) study called The Gulf of Mexico Ocean Monitoring System (*Blaha et al.* 2000). The PI was asked to examine the float data after the floats had been set; when the NOPP study was not renewed the PI sought and got MMS (Minerals Management Services) support to bring the float study to completion. This is a report of that study.

The floats were PALACE (Profile Autonomous Lagrangian Circulation Explorer, *Davis et al.* 2001) ones. They were built by Webb Research of Falmouth, Massachusetts and a PALACE float is shown in **Fig. 1**. Webb Research acquired the float data and made it available to us.

The data is described later, but basically the floats measured currents at $\approx$900 m depth. They also profiled temperature once a week when they surfaced to get positioned by satellites. While the floats were launched in the northern Gulf of Mexico they drifted throughout the Gulf and yielded a unique view of intermediate ($\approx$900 m) depth currents and temperature profiles (depths $\leq$900 m) over nearly a four-year period.

Fig. 1. Picture of a PALACE float. The PALACE float is 104 cm long excluding the 70-cm antenna. Its diameter is 17 cm and it weighs 23 kg.

3.0 DATA

3.1 Background

The PALACE floats in this study had a seven-day cycle during which about 6.23 days were spent at about 900-m depth, about 2.5 hours rising to the surface where they remained for about 11.5 hours transmitting data to ARGOS and getting surface fixes, and about 4.5 hours descending back to ≈900-m depth. The deep drift depth was chosen to approximately match that of expected XBT casts to be made as part of the NOPP study (*Sturges* 2002, personal communication). The floats recorded in situ temperature on their way up to the surface. The floats also recorded the depth at which they drifted for each cycle.

The floats were set between 83°W and 94°W in the northern Gulf of Mexico on the continental slope and rise in water of depth about 900 m and 3,000 m (**Fig. 2**). Eight of them were deployed in April 1998 and the remaining nine were set in August 1998 (**Fig. 3**). There is relatively more coverage in 1998-1999; the last data from the Gulf of Mexico from these floats was in March 2002 (**Fig. 3**). All the surface and subsurface trajectories are shown in **Fig. 4**. It can be seen that there was relatively good coverage over all of the Gulf of Mexico, that only one float escaped the Gulf of Mexico, and that it was not unusual for a float when at the surface to drift into water shallower than 900 m, their programmed deep-drift depths.

Five of the floats, 141, 155, 156, 157, and 162, worked for relatively long periods of time, up to 3 years and 7 months (**Fig. 3**). While two of the other floats (159 and 167) failed prematurely for unknown reasons while in deep water, the others failed prematurely after they drifted in shallow continental shelf waters where they were not designed to operate.

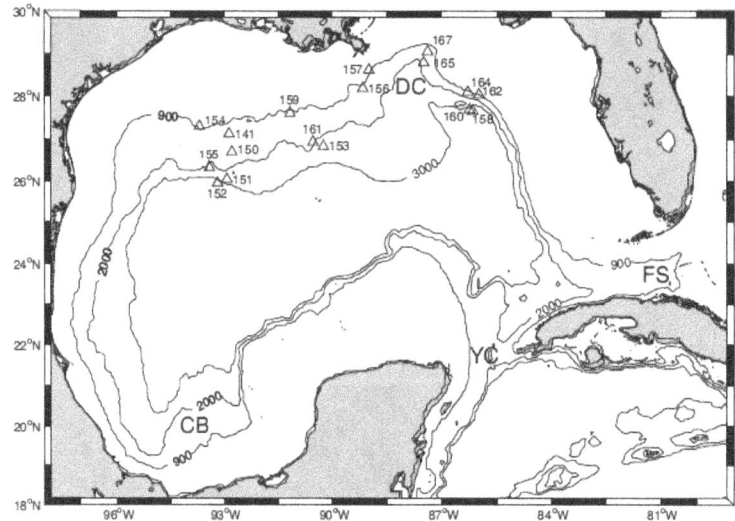

Fig. 2. Chart of the Gulf of Mexico showing the launch positions, the numbered open triangles, of the 17 PALACE floats. The numbering system is that of Dr. John Blaha at NAVOCEANO who acquired and launched the floats. The 900-m, 2,000-m and 3,000-m isobaths are shown. CB denotes Campeche Bay, and the CB is positioned over the Campeche Bump, a relic delta-like feature extending into the open Gulf of Mexico discussed in the text. DC is DeSoto Canyon, YC is Yucatan Channel, and FS is the Florida Straits.

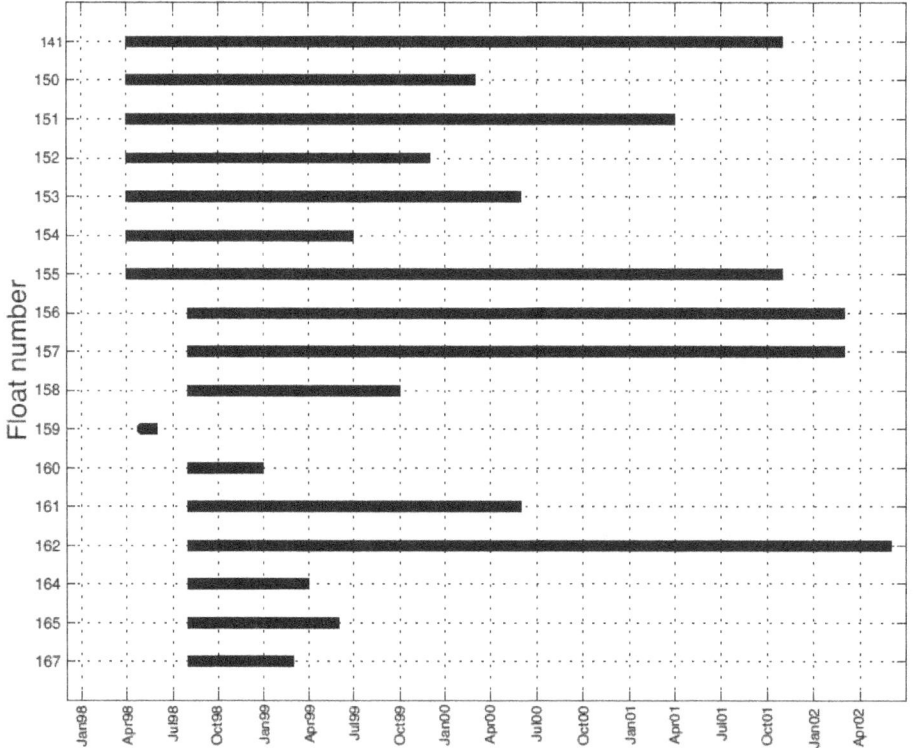

Fig 3. Timeline chart showing when the floats were working.

4

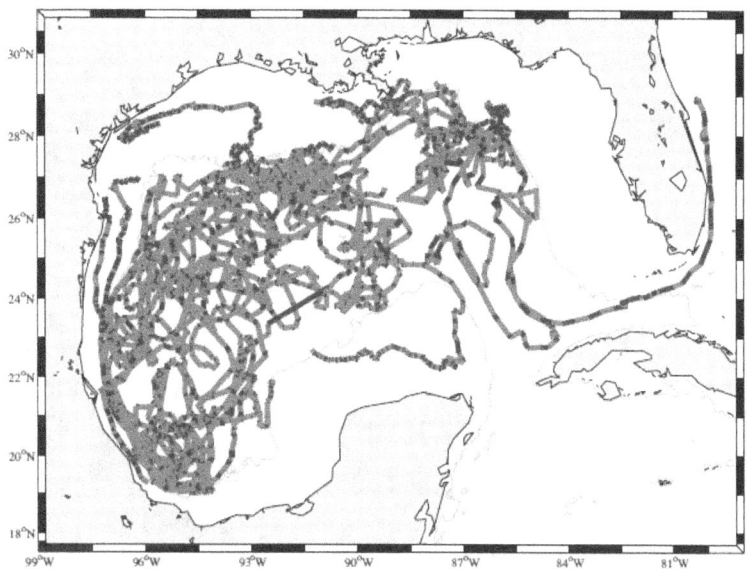

Fig. 4. Surface (blue) and subsurface (red) drifts of all 17 floats. The 900-m isobath is shown. Note the floats drifted at ≈900-m depth.

3.2   Deep Drift Data Processing

In order to compute the deep drift, estimates of surface drift and the drift while sinking and rising were first made using the locations and time of the first and last satellite fixes to estimate the surface drift. Linear extrapolation provided the positions where the floats surfaced and submerged.

A linear decrease of current with depth from its surface value to zero at ≈900-m depth was used to make an initial estimate of the drift during ascent from and descent to the maximum depth. The deep drift was then first estimated. The drift during rising and diving was then re-estimated using the second estimate of the deep drift and the deep drift was then re-estimated. The procedure was repeated three more times. The deep drift speed estimates essentially did not change after the second iteration, and the first estimate was generally within 10% of the final estimate.

All trajectories with depth less than 830 m were then excluded. This depth is less than the initial depth all floats descended and we assumed the float had grounded if its depth was shallower than this value. Then depth was plotted as a function of time for each float. Relatively shallow values were checked to see if they occurred near the 900 m isobath; if they did we assumed grounding had then occurred and the associated deep drifts were excluded. Using these criteria 1,315 deep drifts were judged as good and are subsequently examined here. The deep velocity data inferred from these deep drifts are available on the web at http://ocean.fsu.edu/~georges/temps/gomvelocities.htm. We expect to maintain this web site through 2004.

The floats drifted deeper with increasing time at a rate of about 23 m/yr ± 10 m/yr. So, towards the beginning of the study the floats drifted around 900 m depth and towards the end of the study they were drifting nearly 100 m deeper. The depths of the deep drift records varied from 847 m to 1042 m. Because the geostrophic shear in this depth range is relatively weak (*DeHaan* 2002) all the deep drifts are considered collectively here.

What are presented here are the deep drift velocities estimated from the deep drifts and when shown in figures the mid-point of the vector is at the mid-point of the deep drift vector.

3.3 Temperature Data

The floats sampled temperature once a week every ≈5 m in the upper 100 m and every ≈10 m for depths >100 m as they rose to the surface. The thermistors resolved temperature to about 0.002°C - 0.004°C (*Sherman* 2002, personal communication) and can be calibrated to a precision of about 0.005°C (*Davis et al.* 2001). The thermistors were not calibrated but we think their precision is about 0.05°C. In this report the precision is of more concern than the accuracy.

All temperature profiles made in the open Gulf of Mexico in water of depth >200 m are considered, and there were 1,481 of them. These profiles were made throughout the Gulf of Mexico with relatively many of them being made where the floats were launched and in the Bay of Campeche (identified in **Fig. 2**) where some floats tended to aggregate (**Fig. 5**). These profiles can be seen individually and collectively in 1° latitude by 1° longitude bins on the web at http://www.ocean.fsu.edu/~georges/temps/, and we intend to maintain this site through 2004.

Towards the end of their lifetimes some temperature profiles terminated at depths ≈700 m with a suspicious-looking spike; these profiles were excluded. Also, as the floats drifted deeper with time (Section 3.2) they profiled temperature sometimes only below depth ≈50 m.

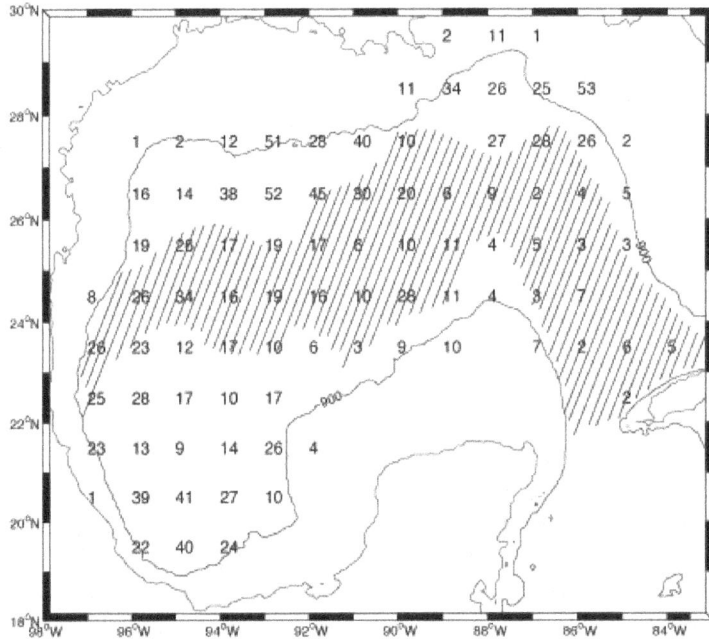

Fig. 5. Chart of the Gulf of Mexico showing the number of temperature profiles taken in 1° latitude by 1° squares. The 900-m isobath is shown. As the number of deep drifts is nearly the same as that of the number of temperature profiles, this also indicates approximately the number of deep drifts in 1° by 1° bins. The shaded area is where temperature profiles were made in the Loop Current and in Loop Current rings.

6

4.0   RESULTS

4.1   Deep Currents

When the individual floats sampled the deep drifts is shown in **Fig. 6**. The gaps in this figure compared to **Fig. 3**, which shows when these floats worked, are primarily due to grounding, i.e. the floats settling on the bottom after resubmerging. A very few of the gaps are due to failure to get a second satellite fix when at the surface; when this occurred the surface drift could not be estimated.

All the 1,315 deep velocities are shown in **Fig. 7**. The vectors are color coded to show where they were launched. The black vectors, from floats launched east of 88°, show a tendency for those floats to remain in the eastern Gulf of Mexico, and similarly the red vectors, from floats launched west of 88°W tend to remain in the western Gulf. It is interesting that some Gulf of Mexico numerical model results tracking particles set to drift at 1,000 m depth show that there is also little communication between the eastern and western Gulf (*Welsh* 2002, personal communication).

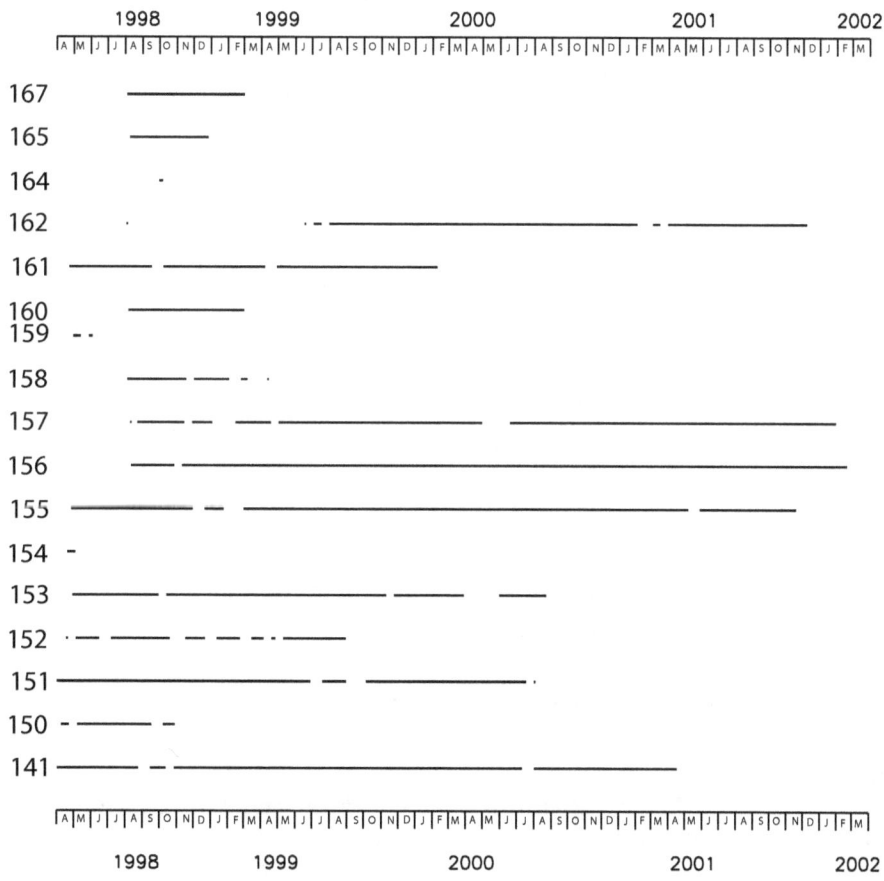

Fig. 6.   Timeline chart showing when the floats worked and obtained deep drifts. The main difference in the timelines shown here and in Fig. 3 is due to grounding (see text).

7

Some patterns are seen in the figure:

- a tendency for counterclockwise, cyclonic flow on the continental margin of the northern and western Gulf of Mexico and in the Bay of Campeche,
- an intensification of the above cyclonic flow in the western Bay of Campeche,
- a tendency for the above cyclonic flow to follow the Campeche Bump in the southern Bay of Campeche (this bump is identified in Fig. 2's caption and the CB in **Fig. 2** is over this topographic feature),
- a small ≈100-km diameter cyclonic gyre in the southwestern Bay of Campeche centered near 20°N, 95.5°W, and two larger ≈300-km diameter cyclonic gyres one in the southwestern Gulf of Mexico centered near 23°N, 94°W and the other centered near 27°N, 91°W.

The same patterns are better evident when the same data are averaged in 0.5° latitude by 0.5° longitude bins (**Fig. 8**). Note that to get better coverage the above averaging in **Fig. 8** is done for boxes centered every 1/4° latitude by every 1/4° longitude.

We estimated the statistical uncertainty in the velocity values shown in **Fig. 8** by assuming the integral time scale for velocity fluctuations was 10 days and using methods outlined in *Weatherly et al.* (2000). The associated uncertainty ellipses for every other velocity vector shown in **Fig. 8** (the figure is messy if all are shown) are plotted in **Fig. 9** *provided the number of values used to form the estimate $n \geq 5$*. As can be seen the velocity estimates for $n \geq 5$ are generally significant in that at least the direction of the flow is resolved. **Fig. 10** is Fig. 8 redone showing only those averages formed with for $n \geq 5$. The velocity patterns noted above survive in **Fig. 10**.

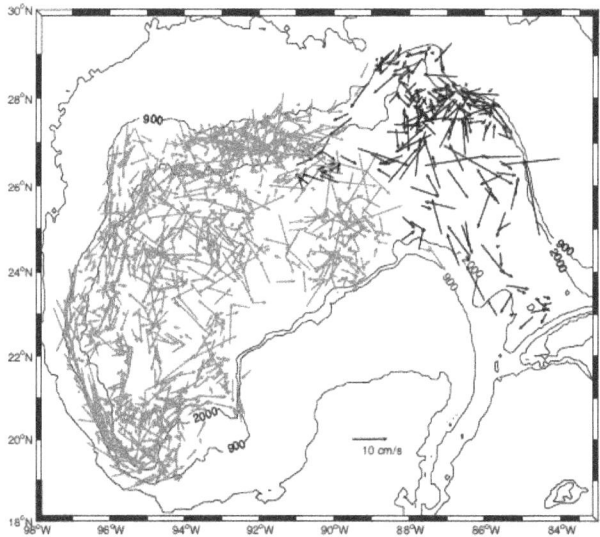

Fig. 7. The 1,315 ≈900-m depth velocity vectors obtained from the floats. The floats launched east of 89°W are black, and those launched west of 89°W are red. The 900-m and 2,000-m isobaths are shown.

8

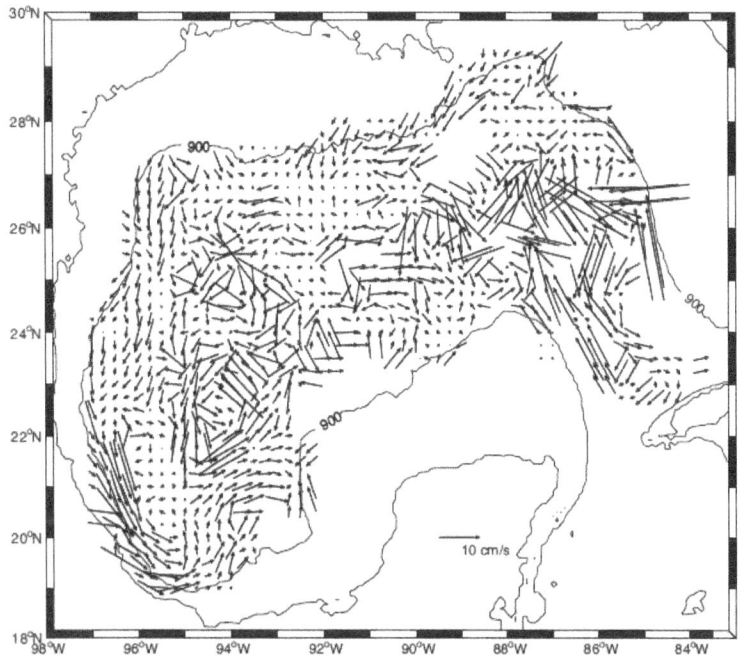

Fig. 8. 1/2° by 1/2° averaged velocities. The vectors are centered in the middle of the boxes, and values are shown for boxes centered every 1/4° by 1/4°. The 900-m isobath is shown.

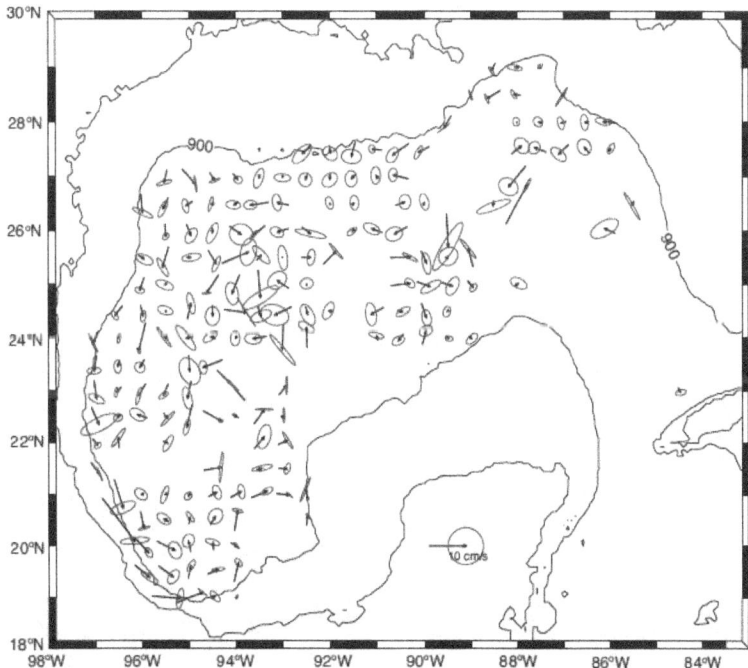

Fig. 9. Average velocity vectors in Fig. 8 with uncertainty ellipses (see text). Every other vector is shown provided the number of estimates *n* used to form the vector was greater than 5 (see text). For $n \geq 5$ generally the direction of the flow is resolved and statistically significant.

To estimate when the flow features noted above were sampled during the ≈3.8-year study period when deep drifts were obtained (Fig. 6) the deep velocities were drawn for sequential six-month periods. These figures are shown in **Appendix A** and **Table 1** summarizes the results. The cyclonic flow along the slope does appear to be a feature of the flow during the period of study. It is least conclusive in the northeast (NE) Gulf where the sampling was the least of all the (a) regions. The intensification of the cyclonic flow along the western Campeche Bay (WCB) appears as a rigorous feature; every time a float went through this region strong southerly flow was experienced at least part way through its transit of the region. The cyclonic gyres (20, 23, and 27) appear to be there during the four-year study period, and not due to parked, transient cyclonic eddies.

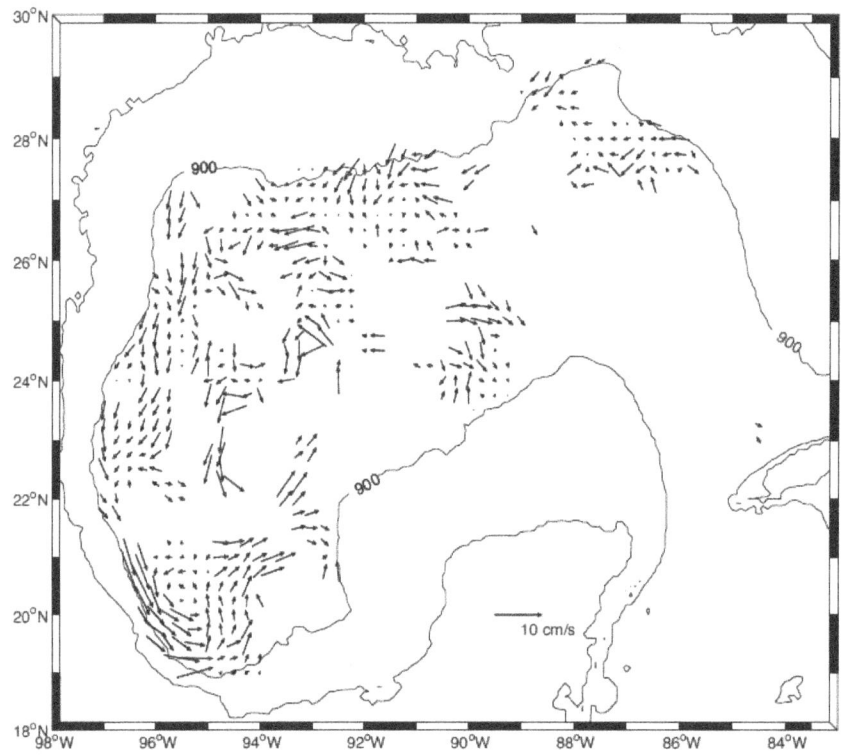

Fig. 10. Fig. 8 redrawn showing only those vectors with $n \geq 5$. The vectors shown here are generally statistically significant.

10

Table 1. Tabulation using the figures in Appendix A of when different regions of the Gulf of Mexico had their deep flow sampled. Under (a) is the continental slope region in the northeast Gulf east of 89° W (NE), continental slope region in the northern Gulf between 89°W and 95°W (N), continental slope region in the western Gulf north of 23°N (NW), continental slope region in the western Bay of Campeche (WCB) south of 23°N, and in the Campeche Bump region of Campeche Bay (CBB). Under (b) are the cyclonic gyres centered near 20°N, 95.5°W (20), near 23°N, 94°W (23), and near 27°N, 91°W (27). An "x" indicates data during the period.

Period	Cyclonic flow along slope					Cyclonic gyres		
	(a)	(a)	(a)	(a)	(a)	(b)	(b)	(b)
	NE	N	NW	WCB	CBB	20	23	27
04/98≤time<10/98	x	x	x				x	x
10/98≤time<04/99	x	x	x	x	x	x	x	x
04/99≤time<10/99		x	x	x	x	x		x
10/99≤time<04/00		x	x	x	x	x	x	x
04/00≤time<10/00		x	x	x	x			
10/00≤time<04/01	x	x	x		x	x	x	
04/01≤time<10/01	x	x	x	x		x	x	x
10/01≤time<04/02		x	x		x			

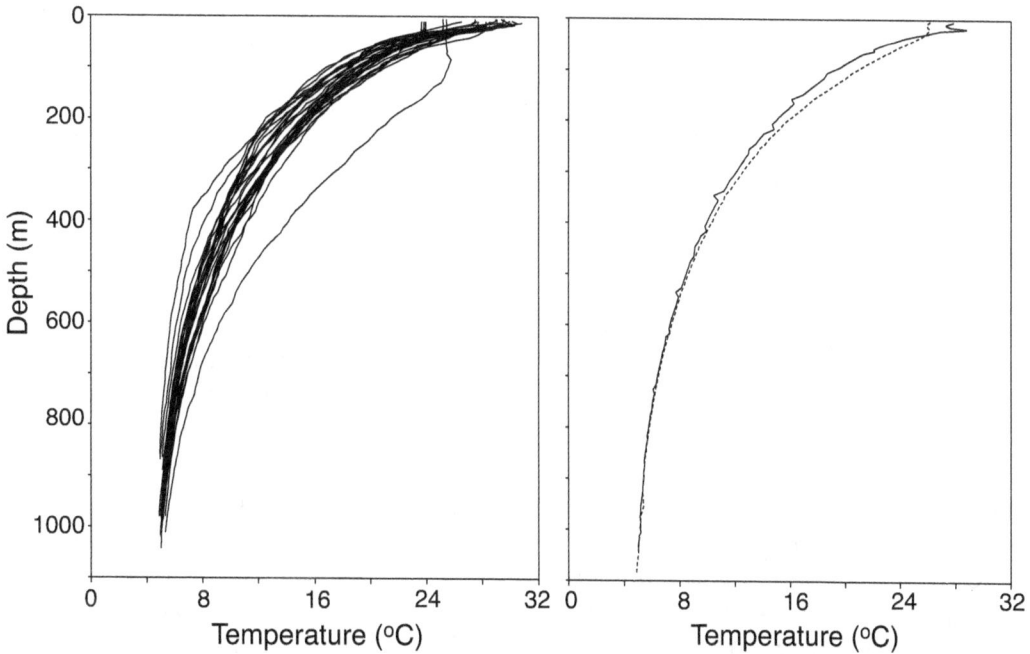

Fig. 11. Left: All the temperature profiles obtained in a 1° latitude by 1° longitude box centered at 27.5°N, 87.0°W showing an example of a profile obtained in the Loop Current; it is the right-most profile (see Section 4.2). Also seen are two profiles obtained in a subsurface cold eddy; the two left-most profiles (see Section 4.3). Right: Dashed curve is the average temperature profile of the Gulf of Mexico from 1,481 PALACE profiles; solid curve is the average profile of those shown in left panel.

11

4.2 Extension of Loop Current and Loop Current Rings to ≈900-m Depth

We superposed velocity vectors on satellite altimeter maps to try to detect patterns between what happened at the surface and what happened at 900-m depth. We used Bob Leben's altimeter maps for the comparisons (some examples are shown later). We tried two variants: monthly satellite maps with all deep currents within 2 weeks of the map and the other bi-weekly satellite maps with all deep currents within a week of the map. The results were inconclusive. The flow at ≈900-m depth sometimes appeared to be a deep extension of what appeared to be happening at the surface. Other times, it appeared to be flowing counter to what the satellite indicated happened at the surface. And at other times there appeared to be no connection between the two. We could not tell ahead what to expect. For example no pattern could be found for flow under the Loop Current, flow under newly formed Loop Current Rings, flow under older Loop Current Rings, and flow under cyclonic rings.

One thing that was of concern to us in the above comparison was whether the floats truly were below the surface feature as indicated by the satellite. A slight shift in the position of the indicated surface feature might give better agreement. Also of concern, if the surface features were generally well positioned, there might be a vertical tilt to the features with depth. To do away with these ambiguities we looked at deep current data when both the temperature data *from the profiling float* and the altimeter indicated that the float had been under and in the Loop Current or a Loop Current Ring. As an example, we show in **Fig. 11** all temperature profiles from one 1° latitude by 1° longitude box taken from the previously referenced web site http://www.ocean.fsu.edu/~georges/temps/, namely the 27-28°N, 86.5-87.5°W box. One profile is conspicuously warm in this box (profile 162168) indicating that this profile was made either in the Loop Current or a Loop Current Ring. Comparing the location of this profile (27.1°N, 86.9°W) with the satellite map for the date of this profile (Jan. 10, 2001) found at http://www-ccar.Colorado.EDU/pub/gom/met/gif.mean shows that this temperature profile was made in this case in the Loop Current.

We found 103 cases when the floats temperature profile and the associated altimeter map for the appropriate day indicated that the floats was in the Loop Current or in a Loop Current Ring. **Fig. 12** shows two histograms of the magnitude of the 900-m depth currents: one is for all the deep current data from the Gulf of Mexico and the other for the 103 values measured beneath the Loop Current or a Loop Current Ring. The currents are indeed stronger beneath the Loop Current and Loop Current Rings implying that in general there is a deep (to at least ≈900 m) extension of these features. Scatter plotting the deep flow magnitude against that at the surface (the latter were read from the previously referenced web site http://www-ccar.Colorado.EDU/~realtime/gom-real-time_vel/, which at the time of this writing no longer exists) that the magnitude of the current at ≈900-m depth below these features ≈20% (with a lot of scatter) that of the surface, geostrophic flow, and this depth is not a level of no motion (**Fig. 13**). **Fig. 14** shows the direction of the flow at depth *relative to the direction of flow at the surface* (the latter being again inferred from the previously reference web site). There are about an equal number of cases when the flow at depth was approximately in the direction of the surface flow and approximately counter to it. We do not see a clear pattern in the relative direction of the deep flow depending on whether the float was on the northern, eastern or western side of the Loop Current or a Loop Current Ring or on the southern side of a Loop Current Ring.

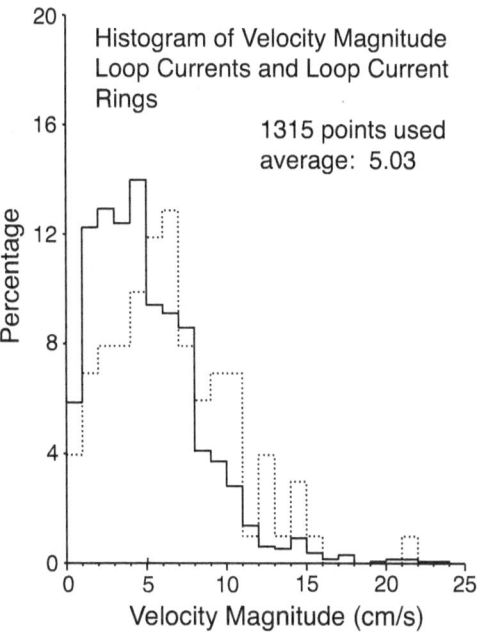

Fig. 12. Histogram of the velocity magnitude for measurements made under/in the Loop Current or a Loop Current Ring (dashed curve) and histogram of all the velocity magnitudes obtained in the Gulf of Mexico (solid curve).

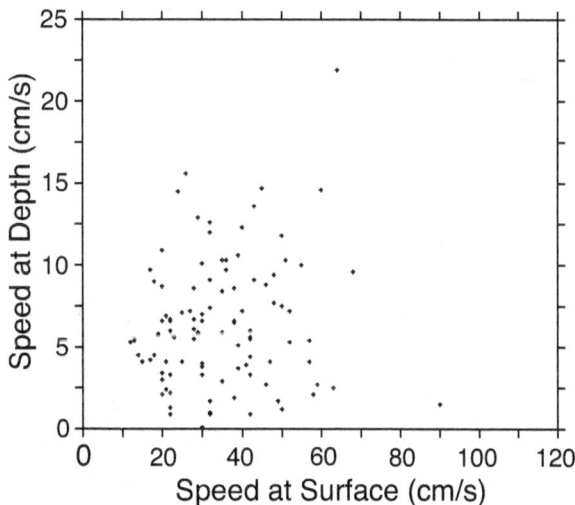

Fig. 13. Scatter plot of the vector magnitude of the current at ≈900-m depth when the float was under/in the Loop Current or in a Loop Current Ring and the corresponding surface geostrophic current (see Section 4.2). The flow at ≈900-m depth was about 20% that at the surface but with much scatter.

4.3 Cold, Cyclonic Eddies and ≈900-m Depth Flows

In **Fig. 11** two cold features are seen -- the two left-most profiles. They diverge from the other, more normal profiles at about 250 m depth and beneath this depth they are notably colder than the other profiles down to the depth of the lowest measurements ≈900 m. We found 38 notably colder profiles and where they were observed in the Gulf of Mexico is shown in **Fig. 15**. Our interpretation is that these features are associated with 13 different cold eddies with 11 of these sampled more than once. In **Fig. 15** where these were first sampled is indicated by an asterisk and subsequent sampling locations, usually a week later, are indicated by solid dotes. These features moved generally westward at a speed of 2-4 km/day (i.e., about 3-5 cm/s) except in the Campeche Bay where they had a southward component in the western bay and a northern component in the eastern bay.

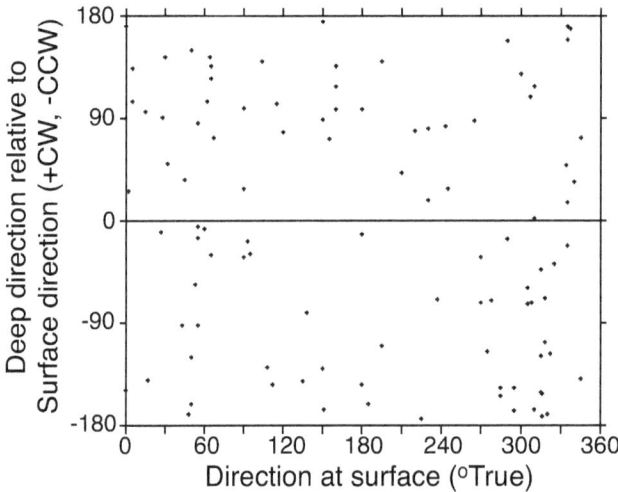

Fig. 14. Scatter plot of the flow direction at ≈900-m depth relative to that at the surface when the float was under/in the Loop Current or in Loop Current Ring (see Section 4.2). Positive values are counterclockwise and negative are clockwise. About half the time the flow at depth was in the direction of the surface flow to ± 90°, and in the other half counter to the surface flow to ± 90° with no apparent pattern depending on the direction of flow at the surface (i.e., on which side of the Loop Current or a Loop Current Ring it was on).

The associated temperature profiles for **Fig. 15** are shown in **Fig. 16**. Some of these cold eddies, 3, 5, 6, 8, 9, 11, 12, and 13, appear to extend up to the surface or at least to the base of the surface mixed layer. Eddy 9 appears to be the one of the cyclonic eddies mentioned in *Zavala-Hidalgo et al.* (2003) (their eddy 8), and like the others are associated with cyclonic eddy features seen in the altimeter maps. The exception appears to be eddy 8; no clear cyclonic feature is apparent in the associated altimeter maps. Cyclonic eddies with a surface expression often drifting westward have previously been reported in the Gulf of Mexico (e.g., the references in *Zavala-Hidalgo et al.* 2003). What may be new here is that in the Bay of Campeche they appear to drift cyclonically about the Bay.

Other of these cold eddies, 1, 4, 7, and 10 are subsurface features; 1, 7, and 10 begin at ≈300 m depth and 4 which is on the upper rise begins at a shallower ≈200 m depth (**Fig 16**). Subsurface cyclonic eddies have been seen before in the Gulf of Mexico (*Elliot* 1979;

14

Hamilton 1992) what is new here is that we have quasi-simultaneous deep velocity measurements in them clearly showing cyclonic circulation at ≈900-m depth in them. **Fig. 17** shows some satellite altimeter maps for the period eddy 1 was observed. The white dashed circle in this figure shows where eddy 1 was and the velocity vectors show clear cyclonic rotation patterns. Also, from this figure a slow drift westward over one month period is evident. The orbital motions in this feature at 900-m depth are ≈10 cm/s (**Fig. 17**); we suspect at the core of theses cyclonic eddies at ≈400 m depth these speeds are notably faster. Note that in **Fig. 17** there is no surface evidence of a cyclonic eddy. The other satellite altimeter maps for the period of the other subsurface cold features also do not show surface evidence of cyclonic flow overhead (not shown).

Cyclonic eddy 2 was observed in the northeastern Gulf (**Fig. 15**) and it is unusual in that some of the profiles show it to have a surface expression and in another it appears as a subsurface one (**Fig. 16**). Perhaps some of the subsurface cyclonic eddies start in the northeastern Gulf as cyclonic eddies with a surface expression and the upper portion of these eddies somehow later get clipped off leaving a subsurface eddy behind.

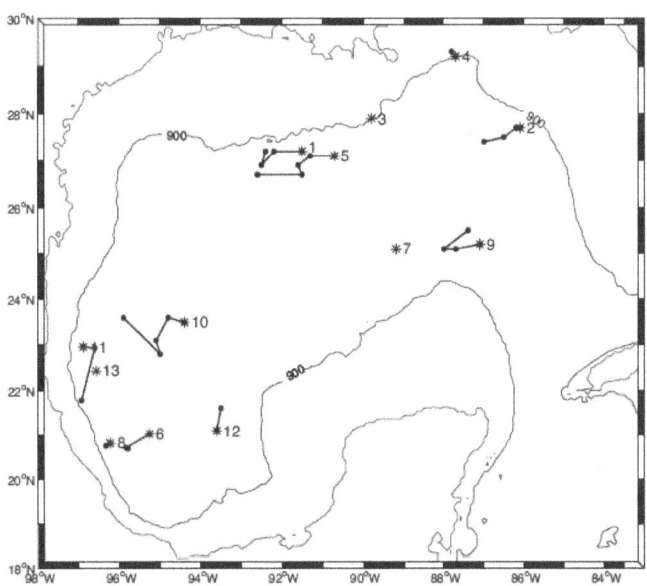

Fig. 15. Location of 13 cold eddies observed from PALACE float data in the Gulf of Mexico. The numbered * show where the eddy was first seen and the site of subsequent observations, when available, are shown with the symbol ● . The lines are drawn according to increasing time. Most of the cold eddies moved westward at about 3-5 km/day, but those in the Bay of Campeche tended to drift cyclonically. Cold eddies 1, 3, 5, 7, and 10 are subsurface rings with no surface signature in satellite altimeter maps (see Section 4.3). The 900-m isobath is shown.

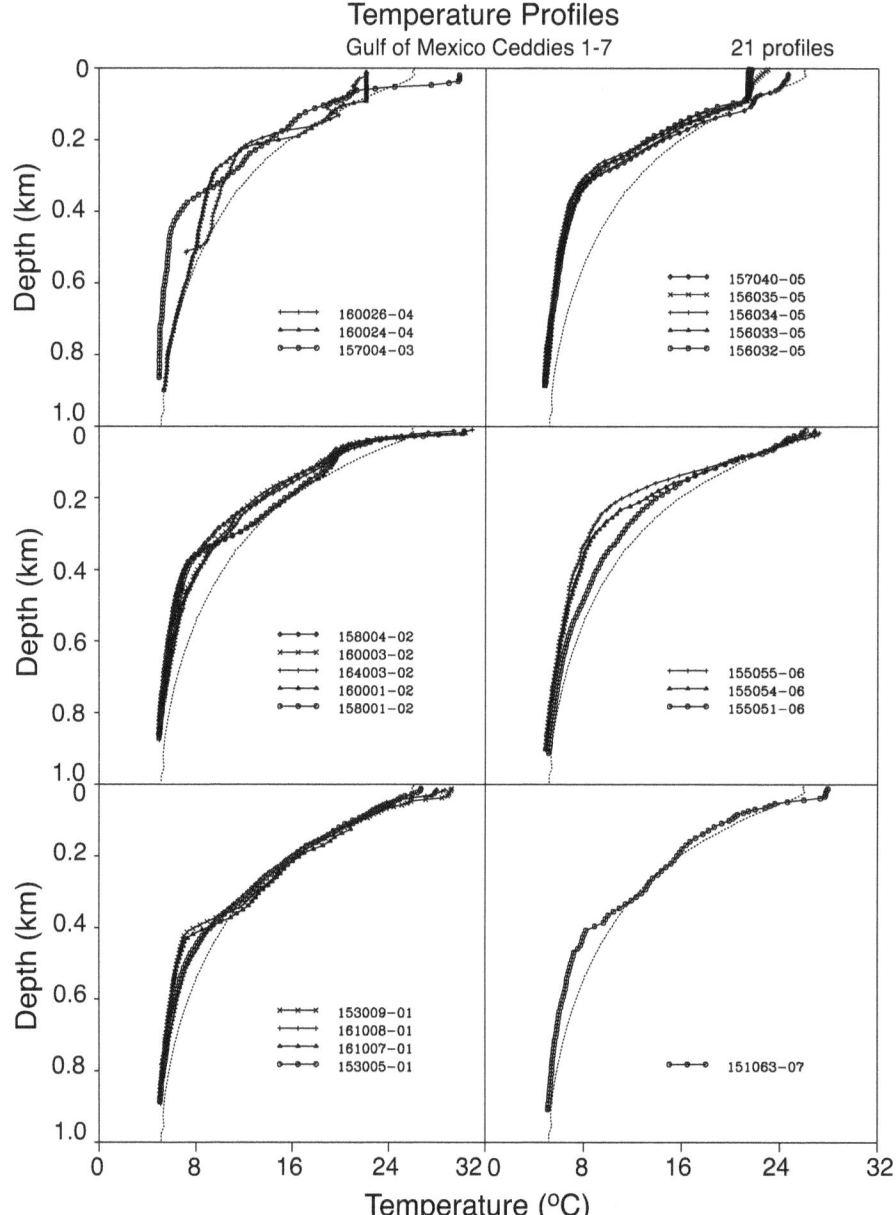

Fig. 16. Temperature profiles used to identify and track the cold eddies in Fig. 15. The last two numbers in each panel identifying each profile are the cold eddy number corresponding to those in Fig. 15. The first three numbers are the float number and the next three the profile number. The dashed curve in each panel is the average temperature profile for the Gulf of Mexico as inferred from the float temperature data.

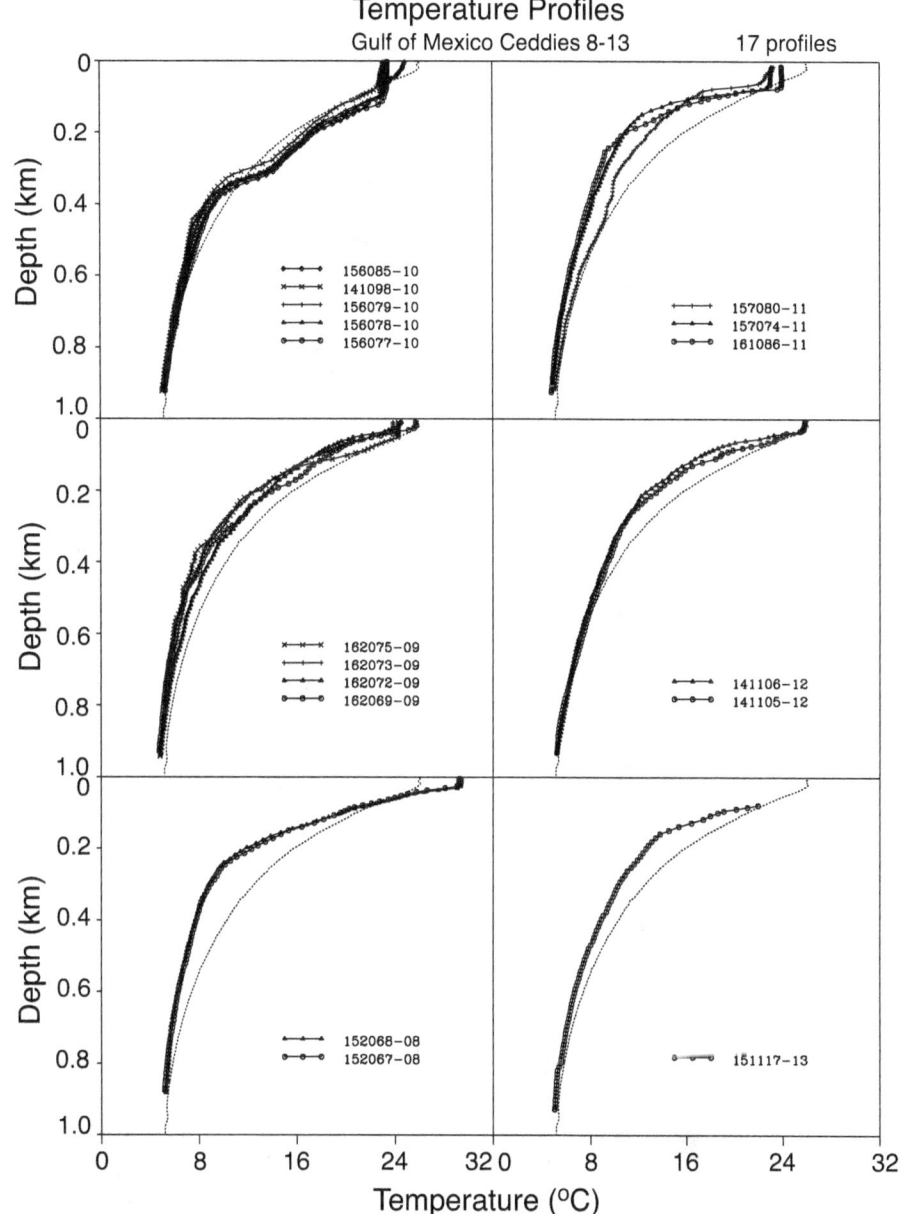

Fig. 16. (continued).

17

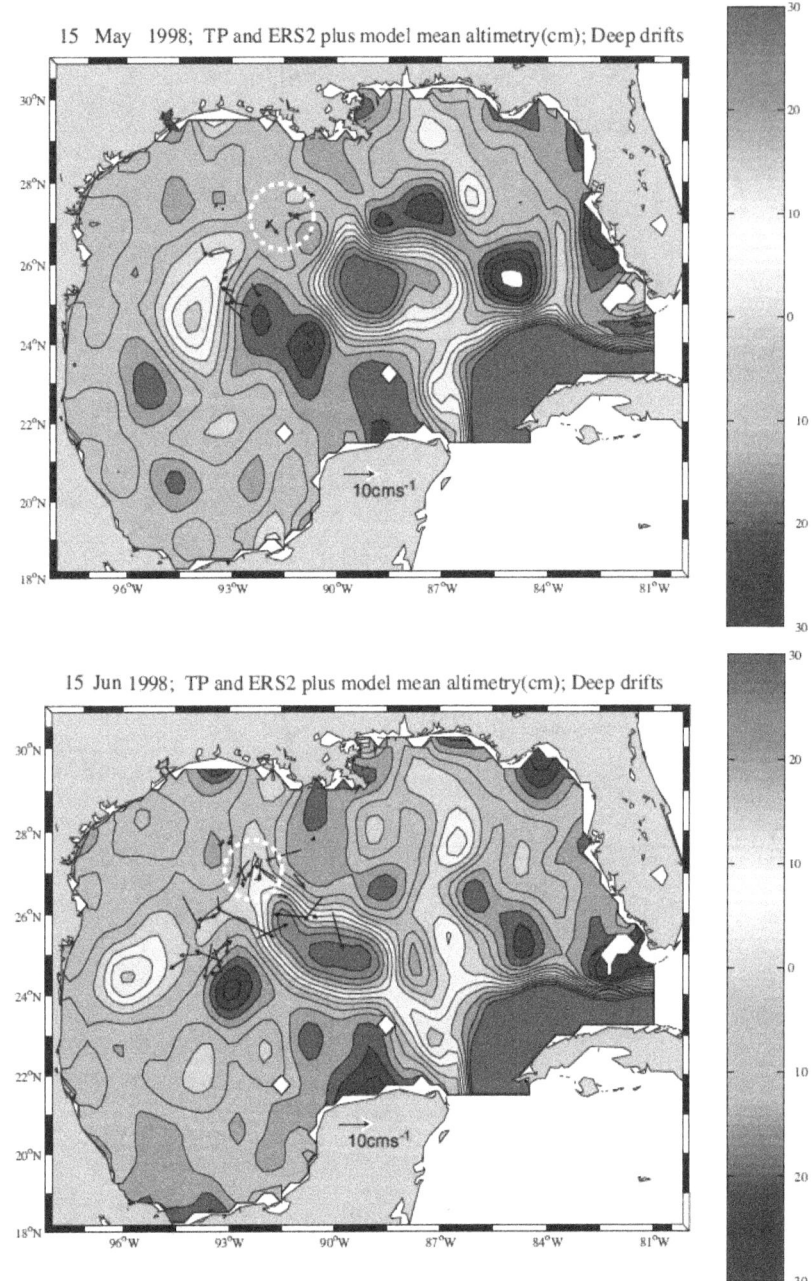

Fig. 17. Two satellite altimeter maps with ≈900-m depth currents superposed. The upper (lower) panel is for May 15, 1998 (June 15, 1998) and all deep currents obtained within ± 2 weeks of the given date are superposed. The white dashed circle show vectors inside cold eddy 1 in Fig. 15. Note that the vectors inside the white dashed circles indicate cyclonic flow and that the eddy moved westward about 60 km in one month.

18

4.4 Temperature Inversions

In examining the temperature profiles for evidence of eddies we were surprised at the number of temperature inversions that were evident. Some examples of these inversions are found in **Fig. 18**. About half (48%) of the temperature profiles had inversions, and these inversions were seen through out the Gulf (**Fig. 19**). About 40% of the inversions were revisited by the same float that first sampled them (**Fig. 20**), and because the floats drifted tens of km between profiles we concluded that many if not most of the inversions were stable features associated with fresher, less saline water and were tens of km across laterally. Because the strongest inversions were found near the mouth of the Mississippi and Atchalafaya Rivers and in the Bay of Campeche (**Fig. 20**), regions which account for about 70% of the river discharge into the Gulf of Mexico, we concluded the ultimate source of these inversions was river water because they should be largest near their sources. Most (96%) of the inversions were found in the upper 160 m, although some were found at essentially all depths where temperature measurements were made (**Fig. 21**).

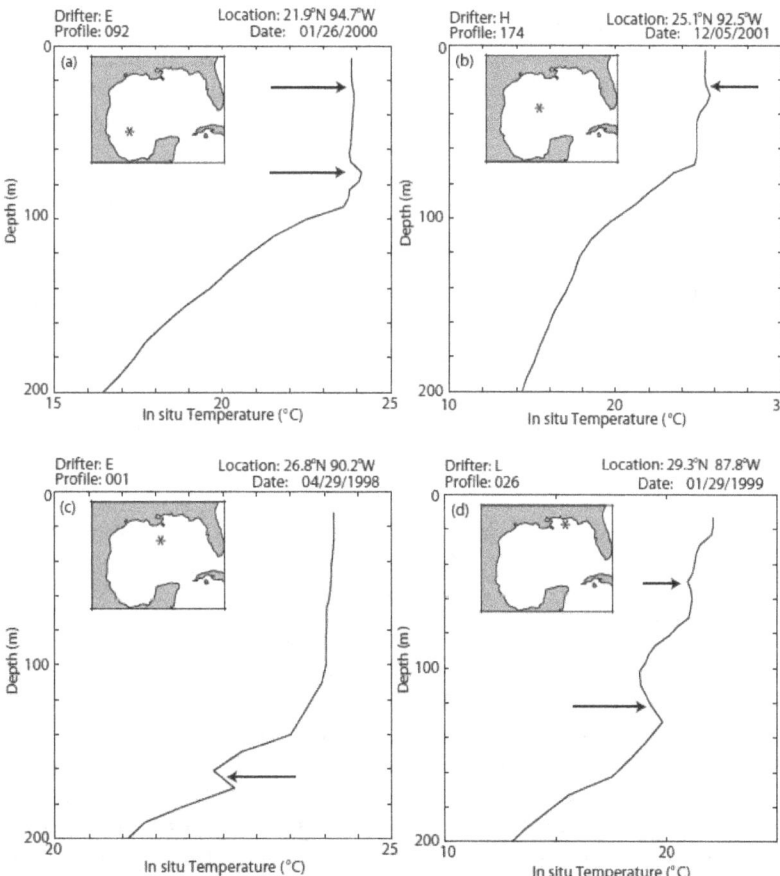

Fig. 18. Examples of inversions indicated by arrows: (a) and (b) show inversions associated with a layer exposed at the surface; (c) and (d) show inversions with a layer isolated from the surface.

19

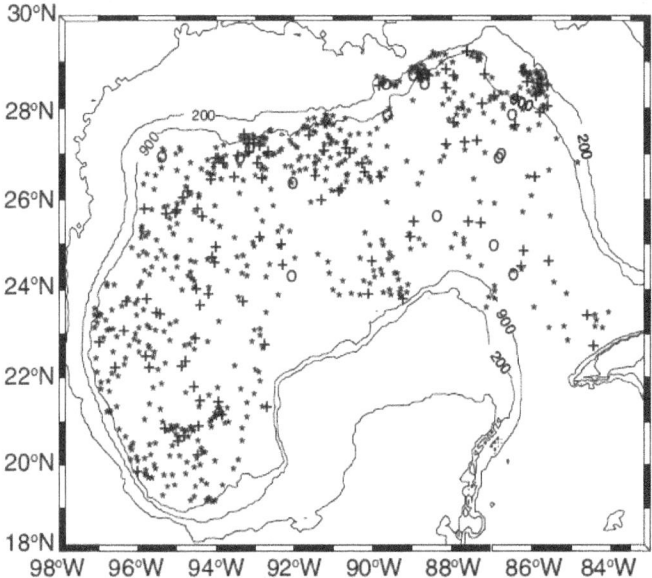

Fig. 19. Location of the profiles showing temperature inversions. This is about half (48%) of the profiles. * indicate one inversion seen in the profile, + indicates two inversions were seen in the profile, and **o** indicates three inversions seen in the profile.

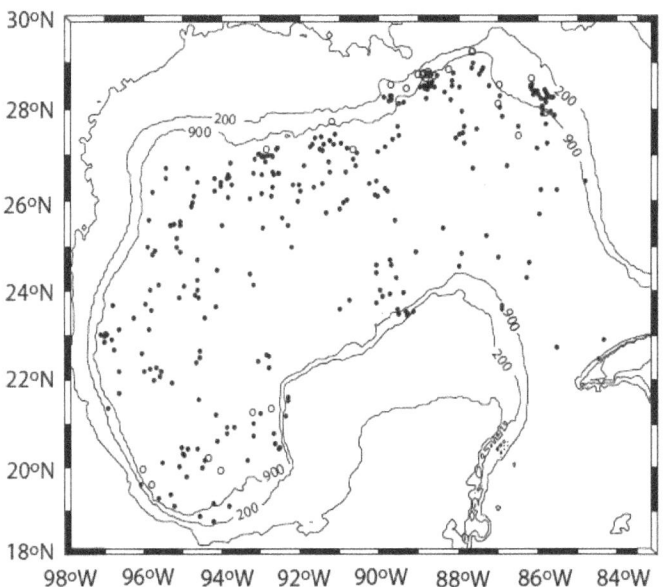

Fig. 20. Dots show the location of profiles with inversions when the next profile from that float also showed an inversion at the same depth to within 100 m. This is 40% of the inversion profiles. From this we conclude that the many inversions are persistent lasting 7 days or more and have lateral scales order several tens of km (see text). The open circles are locations of very strong inversion, $\Delta T \geq 0.50$ °C. These cluster about the base of the continental slope off the mouth of the Mississippi River (at ≈ 29°N, 89.5°W) and in the Bay of Campeche which is in the lower left.

20

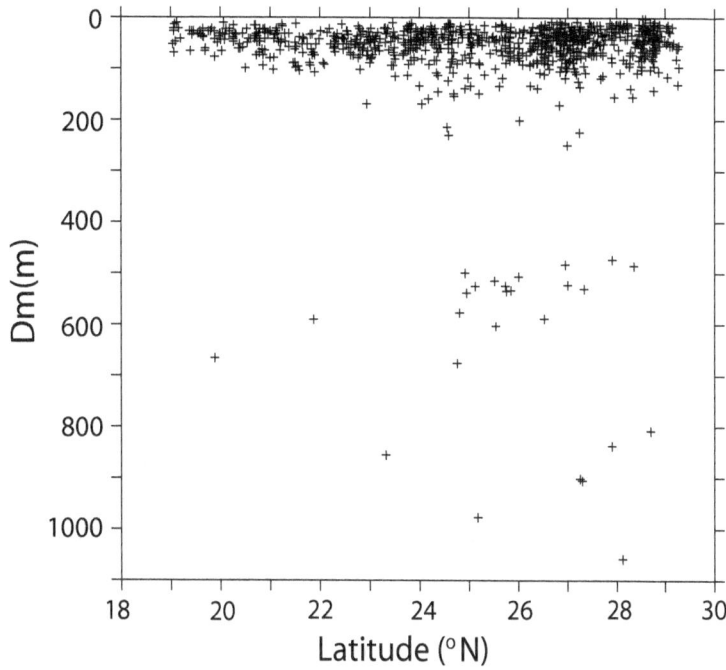

Fig. 21. Distribution depths of inversions as a function of latitude. Most of the inversions (96%) were found in depths <160 m, but some were found essentially at all depths measured by the PALACE floats.

The inversions showed a seasonal variability in that they were relatively abundant in the late fall-early winter and relatively least abundant in the summer months (**Fig. 22**). River discharge of course shows a seasonal variability, but what is of interest is that the time of maximum river discharge is about a half-year before the time of maximum occurrence of the inversions (**Fig. 22**). The explanation for this is given by results from the LATEX, SCULP1, and SCULP2 drogued drifter study (*Ohlman et al.* 2001) which indicates that in the northwestern Gulf most of the river discharge is sequestered on the shelf in the summer months and is ejected into the open Gulf in the winter months (**Fig. 23**) when relatively many inversions are seen. More details on inversions can be found in *Weatherly et al.* (2003) and the profiles showing inversions and details about each inversion can be found on the web site http://ocean.fsu.edu/~georges/temps/inversions/index.htm.

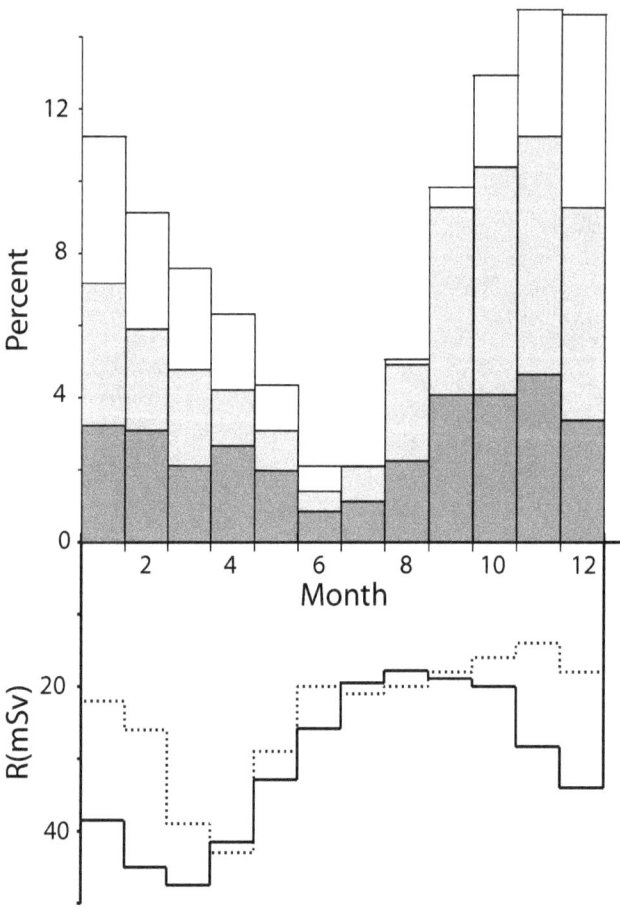

Fig. 22. Lower. Dashed line is the total river discharge in mSV (1 SV = 10^6 m^3/s) into the Gulf of Mexico for the period 10/62-9/65 [from *Hall* 1969]. Solid line is the cumulative discharge into the Gulf of Mexico from 30 U.S. rivers with the mean of Mexican rivers added from the U.S. Geological Survey data on their web site http://waterdata.uscs.gov. Upper. Frequency of observation of inversions observed from the floats as a function of month. The dark, light, and clear color denote the contribution of inversions of strength $\Delta T > 0.050$°C, 0.010°C $< \Delta T < 0.050$°C and $\Delta T \leq 0.010$°C, respectively.

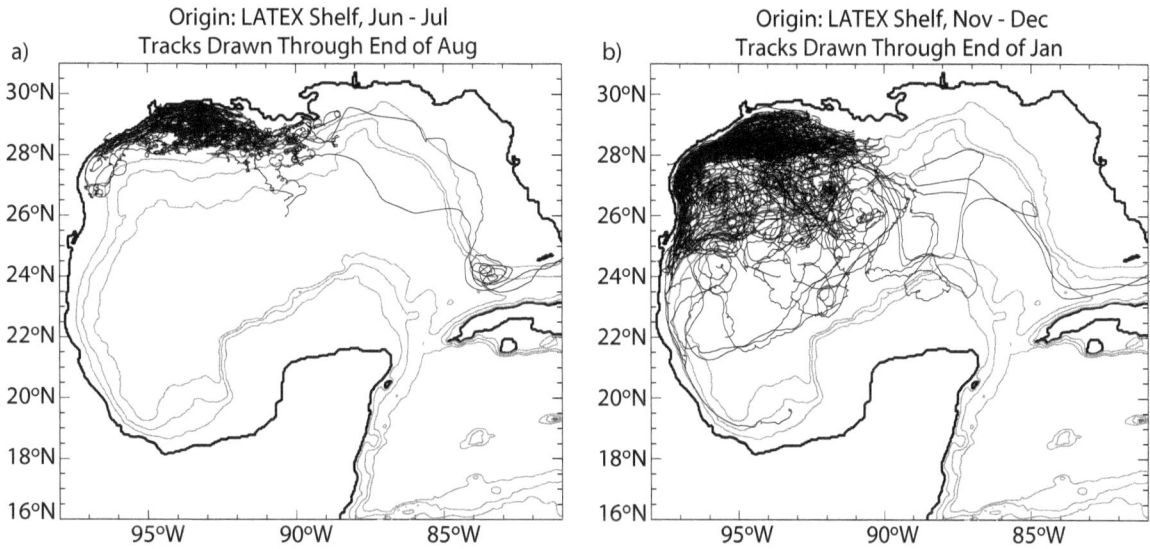

Fig. 23. Trajectories for combined LATEX, SCULPI and SCULPII drogued drifters [see *Ohlman et al.* 2001] for (a) drifters set in the LATEX region (Louisiana-Texas shelf west of mouth of Mississippi River) in June-July with tracks drawn through the end of August and (b) drifter set in the same region in November-December with tracks drawn through the end of January. These figures indicate a much higher probability of finding coastal water in the open Gulf of Mexico in the winter. The 200-m, 1,000-m and 2,000-m isobaths are drawn. Figure is from *Morey et al.* (2002).

4.5 Surface Mixed Layers

In **Fig. 11** examples of surface mixed layers (SMLs) can be found, and most are unremarkable in that they are a few tens of m thick as we would expect. The SML thickness for the profile in the Loop Current (the unusually warm one discussed earlier) in this figure is very thick at ≈75 m. We were a little surprised how thick the surface layer can get in the Gulf of Mexico, and an example of one of the thicker ones, about ≈170 m thick, can be seen in **Fig. 24**. In this section results using the criterion that the temperature in the SML was uniform to within 0.1°C arc presented. Other criteria were tried but the results presented here are not overly sensitive to the choice made. **Fig. 25** shows that SMLs thicker than 50 m were not that unusual, that (as expected) thicker layers occur in the winter months, and that the deepest ones occur not where the surface waters are coldest. **Fig. 26** shows that the deepest SMLs occur in the eastern and central Gulf of Mexico where the Loop Current and newly formed Loop Current Rings are more common, and not in the northern Gulf where the surface temperatures are lowest in the winter. In fact the deepest ones were indeed formed in the Loop Current or in newly formed Loop Current Rings in the winter. Apparently there is sufficient heat loss from the Loop Current and Loop Current Rings in the winter to cause rather deep SMLs.

4.6 Temperature Variability

The 1,481 temperature profiles obtained in the Gulf of Mexico when examined simultaneously show that there is much variability in the temperature at all depths and much variability in the depths of many isotherms (**Fig. 27**). In this section some of this variability is examined and quantified.

The temperature data contoured at the surface, 300-m depth, 600-m depth, and 900-m depth indicates that the Loop Current and Loop Current Rings extend down to at least 900-m depth (**Fig. 28**). This supports the conclusion reached in Section 4.2 that the Loop Current and Loop Current Rings extend to 900-m depth. **Fig. 28** suggests that Loop Current below 300 m depth is shifted about 100 km to the west of the Loop Current at the surface. This apparent shift is artificial and due to the measurements made in the eastern portion of the Loop Current being taken in summer months while those made in the western portion of the Loop Current were made in winter months. No apparent lateral shift in the Loop Current below 300 m depth. It was noted in Section 4.5 that the temperature profiles indicate there is much heat loss in the Loop Current in winter.

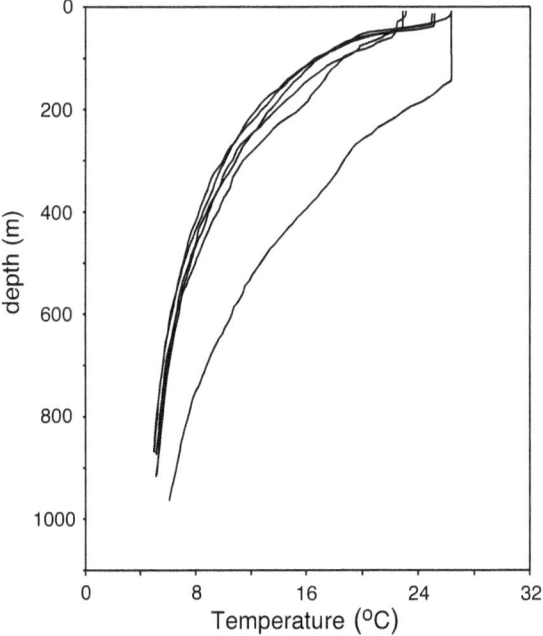

Fig. 24. All temperature profiles obtained in a 1° by 1° square centered at 26.5°N, 89°W showing an example of a very thick surface mixed layer; in the right-most profile which was obtained in a Loop Current Ring in the winter.

24

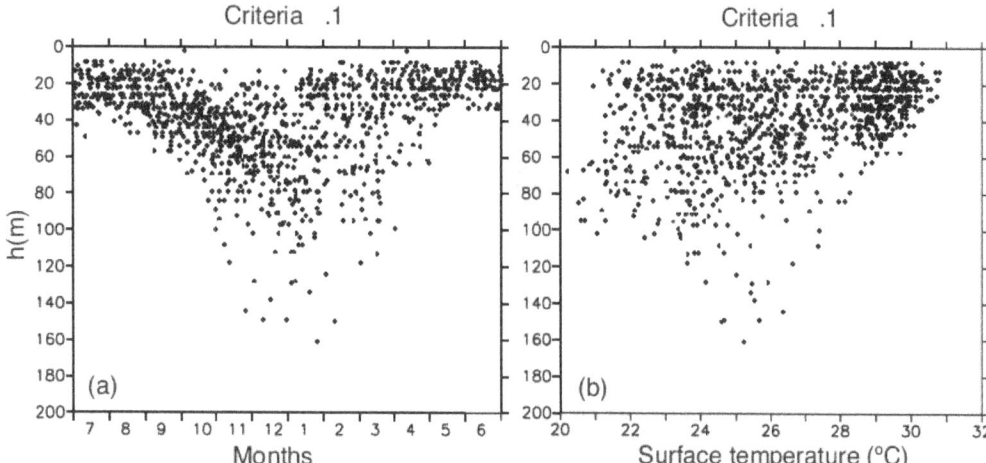

Fig. 25. (a) Surface mixed layer depth as a function of month of the year. Note that rather thick mixed layers, deeper than ≈50 m, are usual in the winter months. (b) Thickness of surface mixed layer as a function of surface water temperature. Note that the thickest layers do not occur where the surface water is coolest.

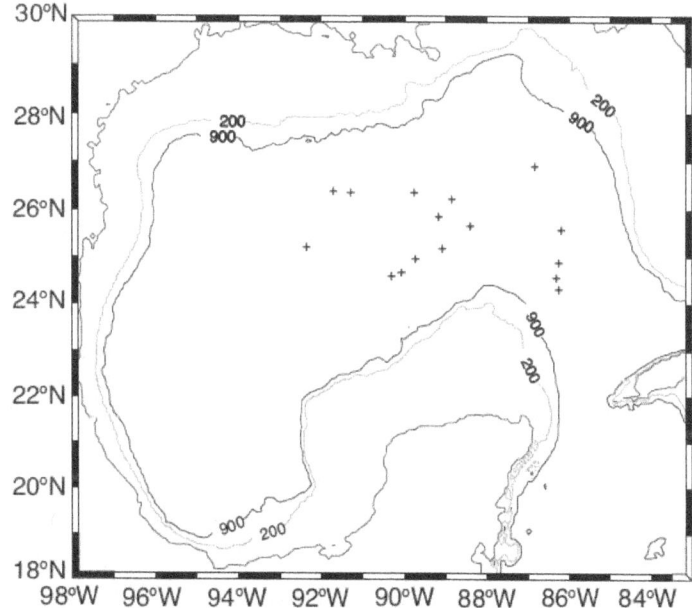

Fig. 26. Location of very thick, thickness >120 m, surface mixed layers. Note that they occur in regions where the Loop Current and Loop Current Rings are common in the Gulf of Mexico. The 200-m and 900-m isobaths are shown.

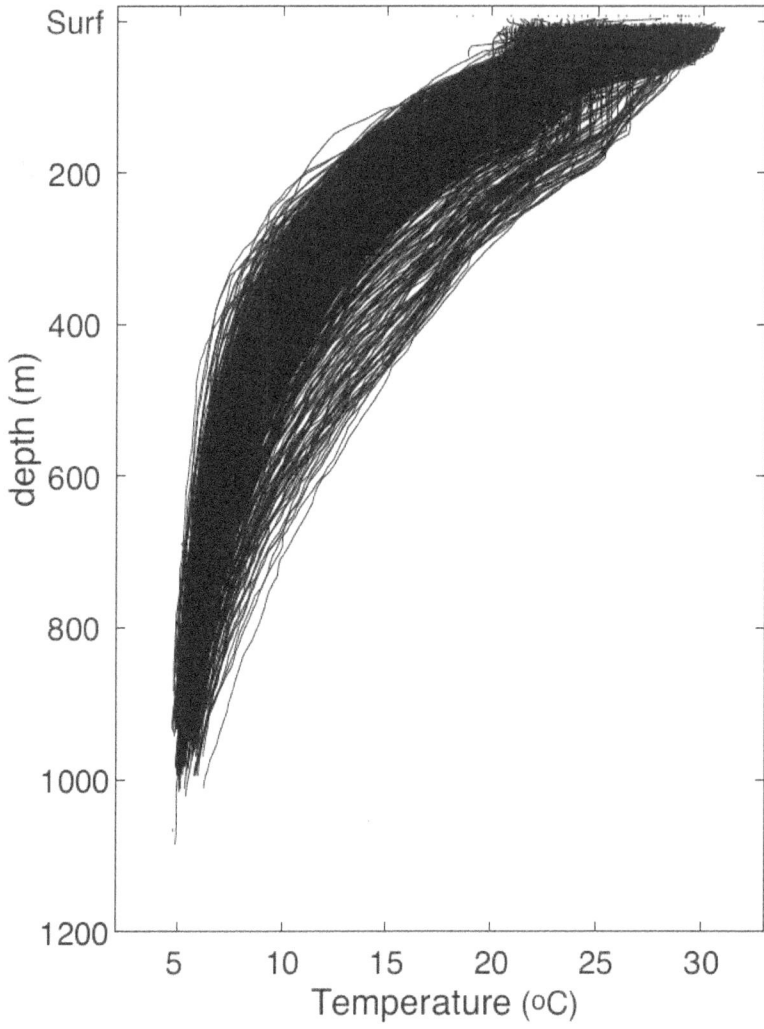

Fig. 27. All 1,481 temperature profiles obtained in the Gulf of Mexico.

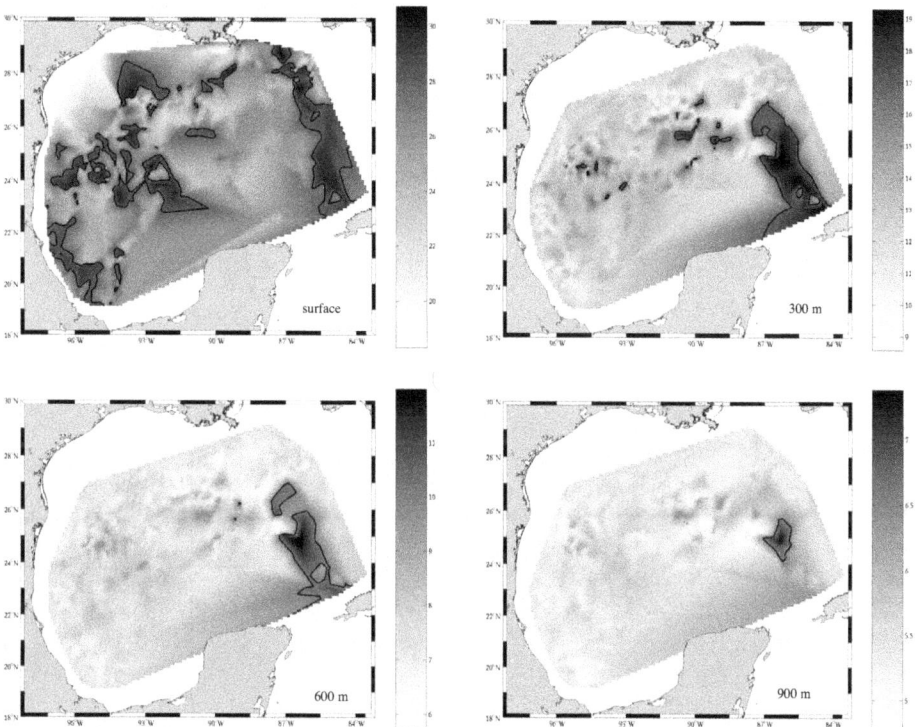

Fig. 28. Contours of temperature at the surface (upper left), 300-m depth (upper right), 600-m depth (lower left), and 900-m depth (lower right). These figures reinforce the conclusion that the Loop Current and Loop Current Rings extend down to at least 900-m depth (Section 4.2). Comparing the panel for the surface with those at depth suggests that the Loop Current shifts westward about 100 km between the surface and 300 m. This is an artificial shift due to when different parts of the surface Loop Current was sampled (see Section 4.6). No lateral shifts with depth for depths ≥ 300 m for the Loop Current and Loop Current are apparent.

It is interesting that in **Fig. 27** the depth of greatest temperature variability is 149 m and that the variability there is 14.1°C (**Fig. 29**). Thus according to the data set examined here the greatest temperature variability in the Gulf of Mexico occurs at ≈150 m depth and it is appreciably greater than that seen at the surface and in the surface layer. It is further interesting that the temperature variability at 300 to 400-m depths, way below the depth of seasonal changes, is comparable to that seen in the surface layer.

Dividing the Gulf into an eastern region, east of 88°W, a northwestern region, west of 88°W and north of 22°N, and a Campeche Bay region, west of 88°W and south of 22°N, the temperature variability is comparable to that of the shown in **Fig. 29**. For the eastern Gulf the maximum temperature variability is 12.7°C and occurs at 188-m depth, for the northwestern Gulf it is 12.2°C and occurs at 168-m depth, and in the Campeche Bay it is 10.0°C at 157-m depth; the figures for these regions comparable to **Fig. 29** and from which these values are taken are not shown.

From **Fig. 27** it is evident that the range of depth various temperatures were measured could be large. For example, the 10°C isotherm was measured between depths of ≈220 m and ≈710 m depth, a depth variation of ≈500 m. The largest depth variation was for the 7°C isotherm and is ≈580 m (**Fig. 30**).

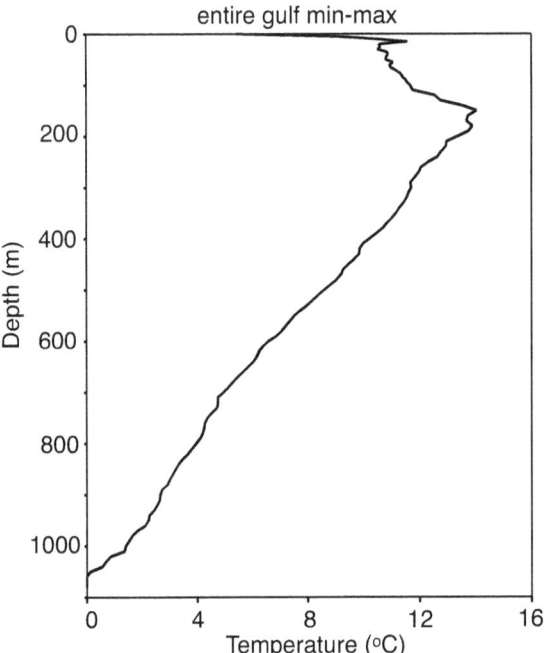

Fig. 29. Temperature variability as a function of depth. The greatest variability is not at the surface or in the seasonally modulated surface layer but rather at ≈150-m depth. It is interesting that at 300-m to 400-m depths, well below the seasonally modulated regions, the variability is as great as in the seasonally modulated surface region. Below ≈150-m depth the temperature variability is likely due in large part to vertical isotherm displacements of transiting Loop Current, Loop Current Ring, and cold core rings.

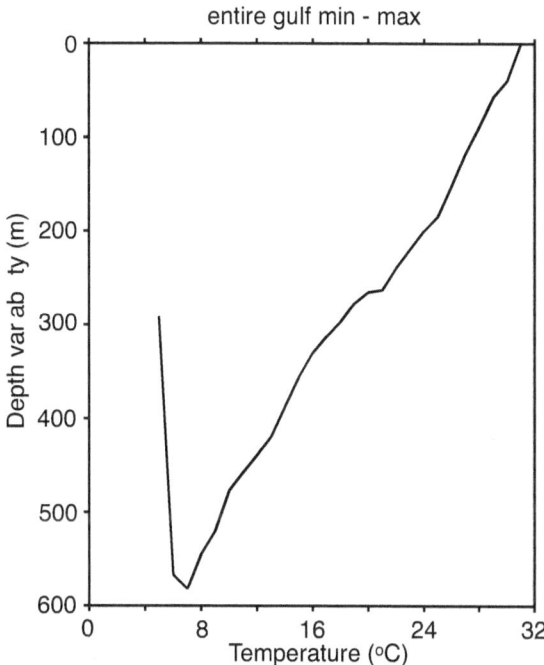

Fig. 30. Depth variability of different isotherms. The greatest variability was for the 7°C isotherm; the depth it was measured varied by 580 m.

4.7 Deep Current Variability

A measure of the variability of the measured ≈900-m depth currents is their variance. The variance of the currents measured in each 0.5° latitude by 0.5° longitude bins is shown in **Fig. 31**. As for the mean velocities shown in **Fig. 9** values are shown every 1/2 degree and only if $n > 5$. Generally along the continental rise and margin these ellipses are aligned with their major axes parallel to isobaths corroborating evidence of topographic Rossby waves there reported in *Hamilton* (1990) and *Hamilton and Lugo-Fernandez* (2001). The ellipses are more circular in the north-central Gulf in the region 26°N-28°N, 91°W-93°W; this may be due to additional variability associated with passing Loop Current Rings in this region. In the central northwestern Gulf, in the region ≈24°N - 26°N, ≈92°W - 95°W, the ellipses are relatively larger and may be due to the previously mentioned deep extension of Loop Current Rings which passed through the region.

4.8 Evidence of Bottom Boundary Layers

By way of background it is rare to see a temperature profile which completely scans the bottom boundary layer (BBL). That is because when CTDs are profiled one usually stops ≈10 m above the bottom for fear of driving the CTD into the bottom and damaging the CTD. Hence the lowest ≈10 m of the BBL are rarely profiled.

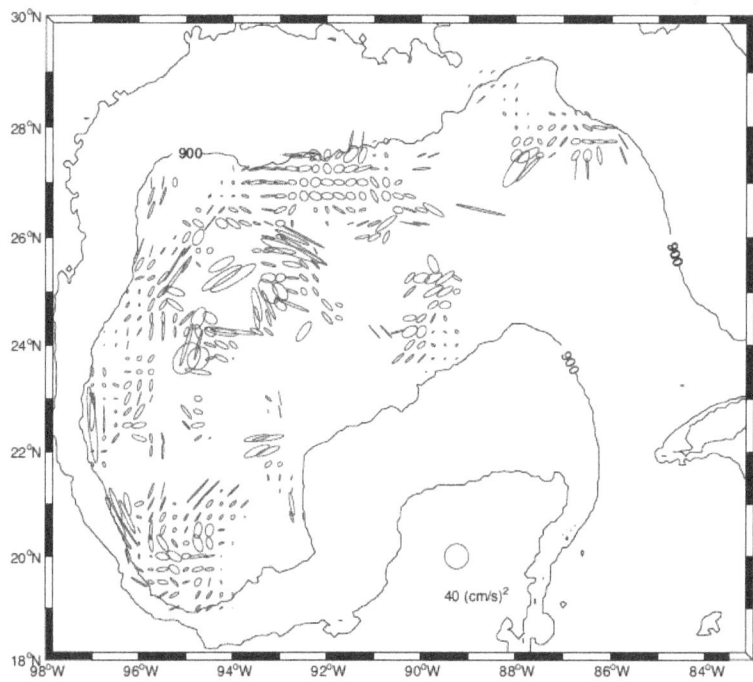

Fig. 31. Variance ellipses for the ≈900-m depth currents. Currents were averaged, as for Fig. 8, in 1/2° by 1/2° bins shifted every 1/4° and for $n \geq 5$, where n is again the number of data used to form averages. Along the continental margin the ellipses are oriented with their major axes parallel to isobaths suggesting topographic Rossby wave activity there as suggested in earlier studies. The variance is larger in the interior where Loop Current Rings transit and in the western Campeche Bay where the southward flowing current there intensifies.

Those temperature profiles obtained from the PALACE floats in 200 m < water depths < 800 m completely profiled the BBL because in these cases the floats started from the bottom where they were grounded. We present a few sample BBL profiles obtained from grounded PALACE floats because they are unusual in that they completely profile the BBL. Of course these float profiles yielded no direct deep current information associated with the temperature profiles because they were grounded. However, from the BBL temperature profile one can infer whether the near-bottom current flowed with deep water to the left looking downstream or deep water to the right looking downstream at the time the profile was made (e.g., *Weatherly and Martin* 1978). In the first case the BBL will appear as a cold bottom layer, and in the second case as a warm bottom layer.

Some BBL temperature profiles obtained in a 1° latitude by 1° longitude box centered at 28.5°N, 86°W are shown in **Fig. 32**. From these profiles it appears that the flow immediately above the bottom on the rise in water deeper than ≈300 m was to the east (deep water to the right looking downstream) and at shallower depths on the rise it flowed to the west. We am unaware of any current measurements made in this region at the time of the profiles were made.

30

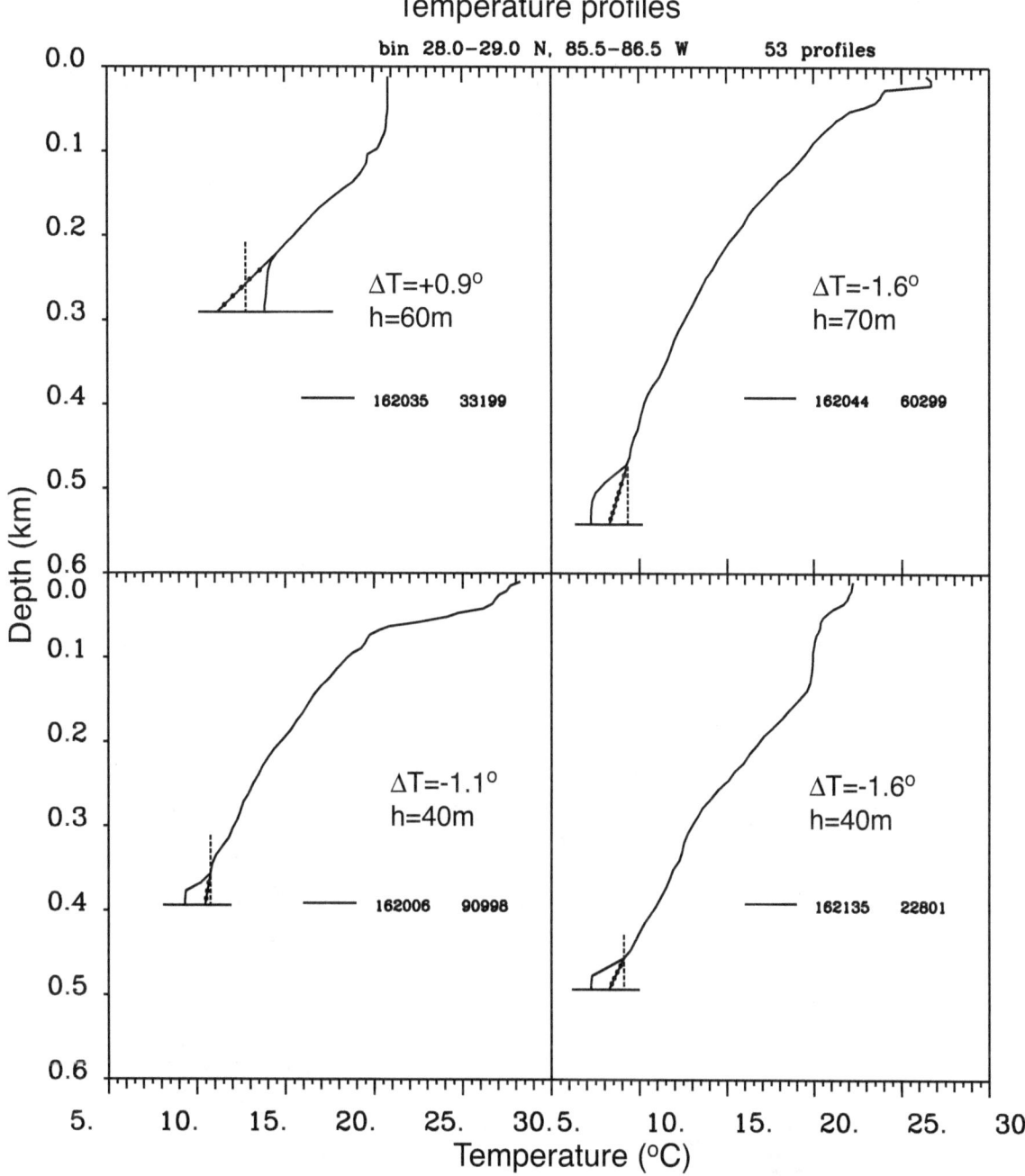

Fig. 32. Four temperature profiles from a grounded float showing evidence of a bottom boundary layer (BBL). The solid curved line is the temperature, the horizontal straight line denotes bottom, the doted and dashed lines are drawn to estimate ΔT, the temperature anomaly of the BBL, and h the BBL thicknesses. For water depth < 300 m (upper left panel) the BBL is anomalously warm ($\Delta T > 0$) indicating here flow to the east above the BBL. For water depths > 300 m (remaining panels) the BBL is anomalously cold ($\Delta T < 0$) indicating here flow to the west above the BBL.

4.9   Comparison of ≈900-m Depth Measured Flows with Some Numerical Model Results

Figs. 33 and **34** and **35** show the average velocity and temperature at 1000 m depth for a one year MOM simulation (courtesy of Susan Welsh), the 3-year average velocity at 1000 m depth from the North Atlantic Sigma Princeton Ocean Model (courtesy of Tal Ezer), and the year 2000 velocity field from the Mercator model (Groupment Mercator) applied to the Atlantic Ocean, respectively. **Table 2** indicates that there is general good agreement with the data.

A feature seen in the model outputs but not seen in **Figs. 8** and **10** is an anticyclonic gyre in the northwest corner of the Gulf of Mexico centered near 27°N, 95°W. This region of the Gulf of Mexico was relatively poorly sampled (**Fig. 5**). Results of an objective analysis we did which produced a non-divergent flow (*Gille* 2003) indicate an anticyclonic eddy in this region (**Fig. 36**). In this figure the red arrows are the results of the objective analysis and the blue arrows are the float data.

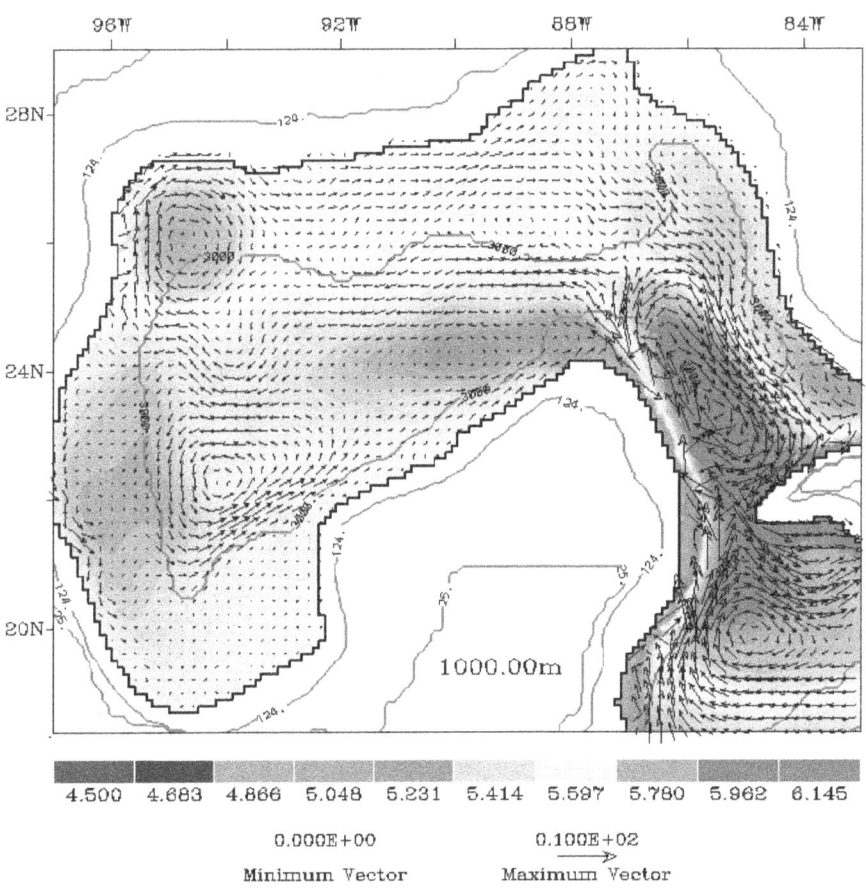

Fig. 33.   Output of MOM model showing temperature and currents averaged over one year at 1,000-m depth (see Section 4.9). For information about MOM see Welsh and Inoue (2001).

32

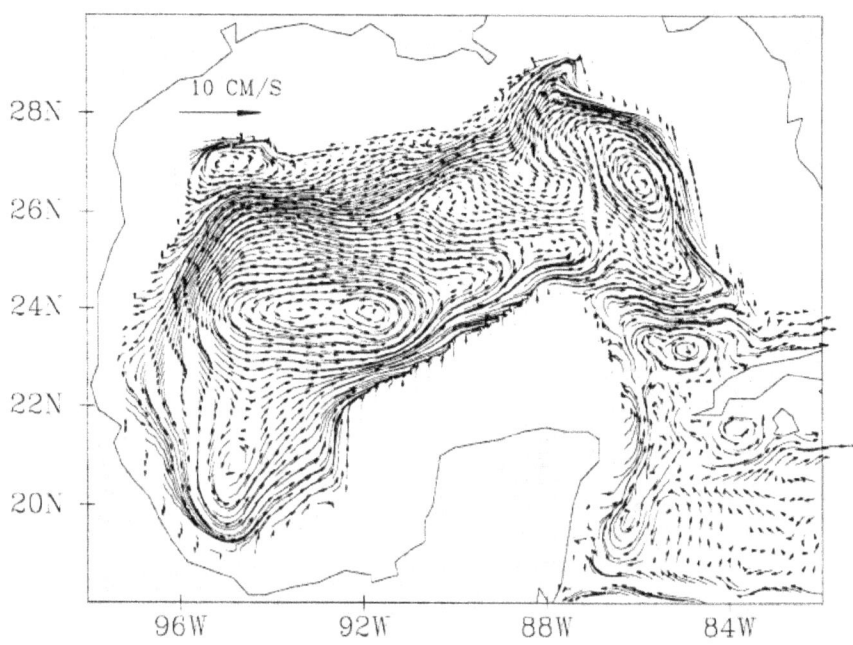

Fig. 34. Average current over a 3-year period at 1,000-m depth from the Princeton POM (see Section 4.8).

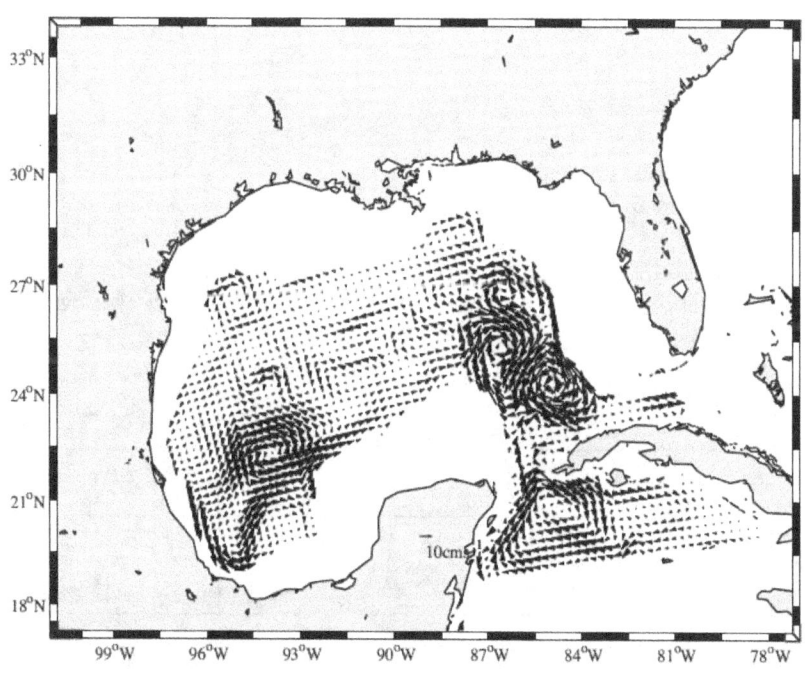

Fig. 35. Average current at 1,000-m depth for year 2000 from the Mercator model (see Section 4.8).

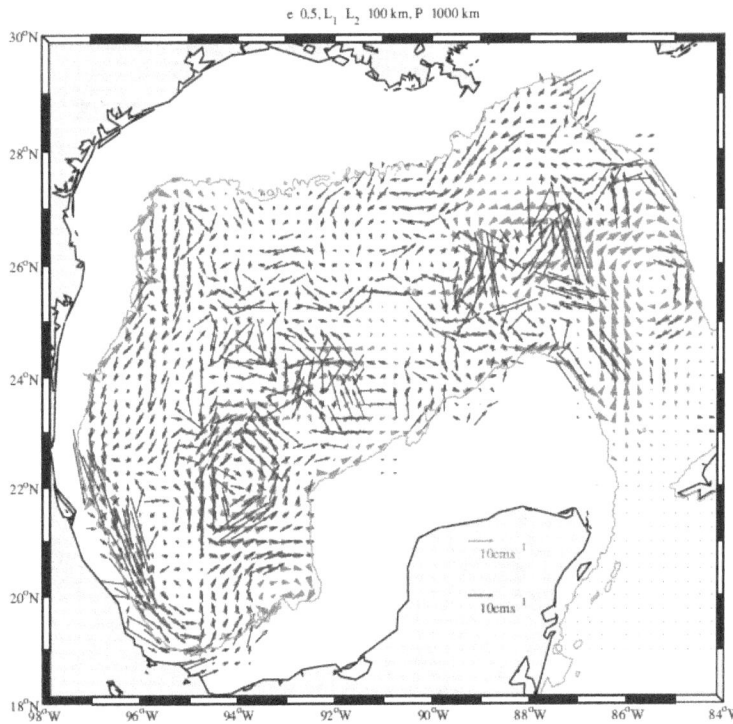

Fig. 36. Horizontally nondivergent flow field (red arrows) inferred from an objective analysis of the actual flow field (blue arrows). The objectively inferred flow field has an anticyclonic eddy in the northwest corner of the Gulf of Mexico as do all the computer model simulations in Figs. 32-35.

Table 2. Whether features seen in float data were seen in model outputs. Under (a) is the continental slope region in the northeast Gulf east of 89°W (NE), continental slope region in the northern Gulf between 89°W and 95°W (N), continental slope region in the western Gulf north of 23°N (NW), continental slope region in the western Bay of Campeche (WCB) south of 23°N, and in the Campeche Bump region of Campeche Bay (CBB). Under (b) are the cyclonic gyres centered near 20°N, 95.5°W (20), near 23°N, 94°W (23), and near 27°N, 91°W (27). An "x" indicates seen in the model output.

Model	Cyclonic flow along slope					Cyclonic gyres		
	(a)	(a)	(a)	(a)	(a)	(b)	(b)	(b)
	NE	N	NW	WCB	CBB	20	23	27
MOM	x	x	x	x		x	x	
Princeton POM	x	x	x	x	x	x	x	x
Mercator	x	x	x	x	x	x	x	

34

5.0 SOME CLOSING REMARKS

The PI would not have chosen 900 m as the drift depth of the PALACE floats. It is too close to the so-called level-of-no-motion (e.g., Stommel 1965). It is also close to the transition depth between an upper layer regime where the flow is dominated by the Loop Current and wind-driven flows, and a deeper abyssal layer as yet poorly understood (e.g., Hamilton and Lugo-Fernandez 2001). Finally, this is also near the sill depth for the Straits of Florida through which the Loop Current exits the Gulf of Mexico. For these reasons the PI expected the mean flow to be rather weak at this depth, as indeed the PALACE floats generally indicated. The only place their data indicated that there was a moderately strong ($\approx$ 10 cm/s) mean flow was along the continental margin in the western Bay of Campeche.

Nonetheless the PALACE data indicated there was a general cyclonic flow around the continental margin of the Gulf of Mexico at about 900-m depth. Whether this is due to upper layer effects or lower layer effects is unknown. Also, the PALACE float data indicated that when there was enough data to estimate a mean current, the mean current was not zero within the uncertainty estimates. So the PALACE data examined do indeed suggest that 900-m depth is not a level of no motion but a region of mean generally weak cyclonic flow about the Gulf of Mexico. This seems an important feature which numerical models should be able to reproduce.

The submerged time of the floats, 6.5 days, is such that the intermediate depth flows they experienced were influenced by strong, transitory flows associated with planetary waves and mesoscale eddies because these flows have time integral time scales also of this length. This study indicates that, for PALACE floats drifting at intermediate depths in the Gulf of Mexico with $\approx$ weekly cycle times, about five samples are needed to average out these transitory flows.

About half of the temperature profiles obtained showed cold layers above warmer layers, which here were called (temperature) inversions. Of these inversions about half were revisited again miles away on the float's next profile. It was concluded this could be only if the resampled cold layers were also less saline layers too, and that they were riverine and coastal waters ejected into the open Gulf of Mexico. Does that mean that the other half of the inversions were due to some other process? Perhaps some were, but it is thought most were not. This is because the tally did not include the many inversions which were sampled on the next-but-one profile. Thus it is thought that most of the inversions are indicators of the presence of riverine and coastal waters rather than mixing processes associate with breaking internal waves and/or double-diffusive processes. If correct, it is unclear what implications the common occurrence of fresh, cool coastal waters far offshore have on the physics, biology and chemistry of the Gulf of Mexico.

6.0 ANNOTATED BIBLIOGRAPHY OF THE PUBLISHED PAPER AND WEB SITES

Weatherly, G., N. Winders, and R. Harkema, 2003. Temperature inversions in the open Gulf of Mexico. *J. Geophys. Res.* **108**, doi:10.1029/2002JC001680.

This paper reports on evidence of riverine water found in the open Gulf of Mexico from the temperature profile data obtained by the PALACE floats. Half of the profiles showed evidence of riverine water throughout the Gulf of Mexico and at all times. It was an unexpected result to see so many and to see them everywhere. We document that the major sources of these fresh layers are the Mississippi and Atchalafaya Rivers, which account for ≈60% of the freshwater inflow to the Gulf of Mexico, and 19 Mexican rivers discharging into the Campeche Bay, which account for another ≈20% of the fresh water inflow. Most of the layers were found near the surface but a few were found at essentially all depths. It is unclear if the deeper ones are due to possible downwelling of the surface fresh layers, double diffusion processes acting to sink the fresh surface layers, and/or lateral advection from the Caribbean Sea of deep waters rich in Antarctic intermediate water.

Note that the following web sites are all linked. We expect to maintain them through the end of 2004.

The web site http://ocean.fsu.edu/~georges/temps/index.htm lists the velocity values inferred at ≈900-m depth for each PALACE float. It is intended as an archive of this data and to make it available to those who might want to access it. The data is also listed in MATLAB form for those wishing to look at these data using MATLAB.

The web site http://ocean.fsu.edu/~georges/temps/index.htm is concerned with the temperature data from the PALACE floats. In this site we have made use of material that was on a now discontinued web site which Webb Research use to maintain. In so doing all the material previously on that web page about the PALACE floats is now on this page.

The temperature profiles sorted in 1° latitude by 1° longitude bins are shown as well as the average profile for each bin compared to the average profile for the whole Gulf. It is possible to see individual profiles by appropriately clicking.

Plots of the average over 1° by 1° temperature contour plots at three depths are shown.

The web site http://ocean.fsu.edu/~georges/temps/inversions/index.htm is concerned with the profiles showing temperature inversions discussed in *Weatherly et al.* (2003). How they were geographically distributed in 1° by 1° bins is shown, and by appropriately clicking the individual profiles with temperature inversions can be viewed. Also, where to look for the inversion on the profile and how strong it is are given.

7.0 REFERENCES

Blaha, J., G.H. Born, N.L. Guinasso Jr., H.J. Herring, G. A. Jacobs, F.J. Kelly, R.R. Beden, R.D. Martin Jr., G.L. Mellor, P.P. Niiler, M.R. Parks, R.C. Patchen, K. Schaudt, N.W. Scheffner, C.K. Shum, C. Ohlmann, W. Sturges III, G.L. Weatherly, D. Webb, and H.J. White. 2000. Gulf of Mexico ocean monitoring system, *Oceanography*, **13**:10-17.

Davis, R.E., J.T. Sherman, and J. Dufour. 2001. Profiling ALACEs and other advances in autonomous subsurface floats, *J. Atmos. and Oceanic Tech.*, **18**:982-993.

DeHaan, C.J. 2002. Determining the deep current structure in the Gulf of Mexico, Ph.D. Thesis, Florida St. Univ., Tallahassee, FL. 80 pp.

Elliot, B.A. 1979. Anticyclonic rings and the energetics of the circulation of the Gulf of Mexico, Ph.D. Thesis, Texas A&M Univ., College Station, TX. 188 pp.

Gille, S. T. 2003. Float observations of the southern ocean: Part 1, Estimating mean fields, bottom velocities, and topographic steering, *J. Phys. Oceanogr*, **33**:1,167-1,181.

Hall, C.S. 1969. An investigation of the water balance of the basin of the Gulf of Mexico. M.S. Thesis, Texas A & M Univ., College Station, TX. 39 pp.

Hamilton, P. 1990. Deep currents in the Gulf of Mexico, *J. Phys. Oceanogr.*, **20**:1,087-1,104.

Hamilton, P. 1992. Lower continental slope cyclonic eddies in the Gulf of Mexico, *J. Geophys. Res.*, **97**:2,185-2,200

Hamilton, P. and A. Lugo-Fernandez. 2001. Observations of high-speed currents in the northern Gulf of Mexico, *Geophys. Res. Lett.*, **28**:2,867-2,870.

Morey, S.L., J.J. O'Brien, W.W. Schroeder, and J. Zavala-Hidalgo. 2002. Seasonal variability of the export of river discharged fresh water in the northern Gulf of Mexico, Proceedings: Oceans 2002 MTS/IEEE Conference Biloxi, MS. pp. 1,480-1,484.

Ohlman, J.C., P.P. Niiler, C.A. Fox, and R.R. Leben. 2001. Eddy energy and shelf interactions in the Gulf of Mexico, *J. Geophys. Res.*, **106**:2,605-2,620.

Stommel, H. 1965. *The Gulf Stream*, Cambridge University Press, London, 2nd edition, 248 pp.

Welsh, S. and M. Inoue. 2000. Loop current rings and the deep circulation in the Gulf of Mexico, *J. Geophy. Res.*, **105**:16,951-16,959.

Weatherly, G. and P. Martin. 1978. On the structure and dynamics of the ocean bottom boundary layer, *J. Phys. Oceanogr.*, **8**:557-570.

Weatherly, G., N. Wienders, and R. Harkema. 2003. Temperature inversions in the open Gulf of Mexico, *J. Geophys. Res.* **108**(C6):10.1029/2002JC001680.

Weatherly, G.L., Y.Y. Kim, and E. Kontar. 2000. Eulerian measurements of the North Atlantic deep water deep western boundary current at 18°S. *J. Phys. Oceanogr.*, **30**:971-986.

Zavala-Hidalgo, J., S.L. Morey, and J.J. O'Brien. 2003. Cyclonic eddies northeast of the Campeche Bank from altimetry data, *J. Phys. Oceanogr.*, **33**:623-629.

8.0 APPENDIX A

The following figures are the PALACE velocity vectors in 6-month intervals and were used in determining **Table 1**. The first is for 04/98 ≤ time < 10/98, the second for 10/98 ≤ time < 04/99, the third for 04/99 ≤ time < 10/99, the fourth for 10/99 ≤ time < 04/00, the fifth for 04/00 ≤ time < 10/00, the sixth for 10/00 ≤ time < 04/01, the seventh for 04/01 ≤ time < 10/01, and the seventh for 10/01 ≤ time < 04/02.

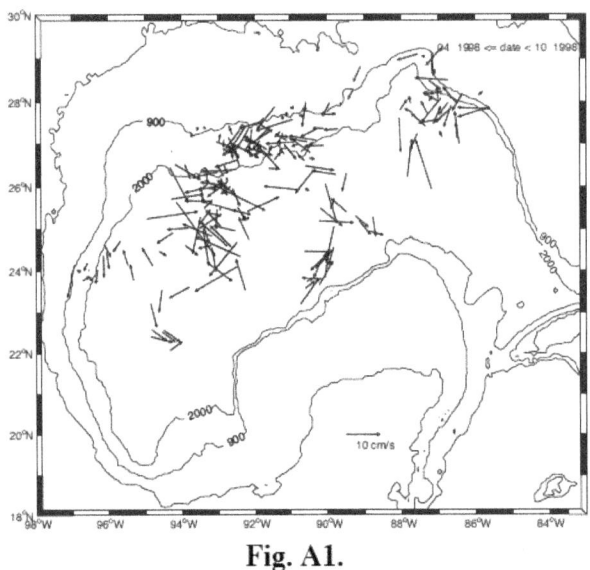

Fig. A1.

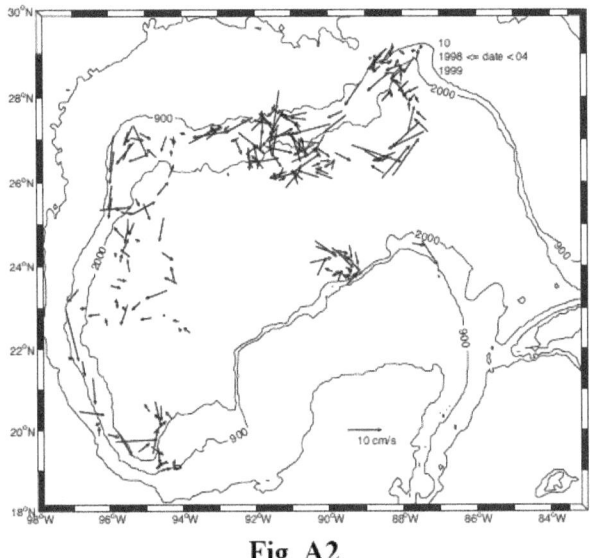

Fig. A2.

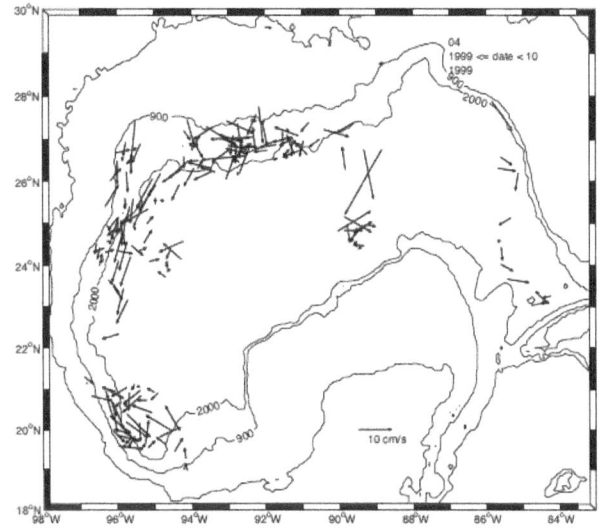

Fig. A3.

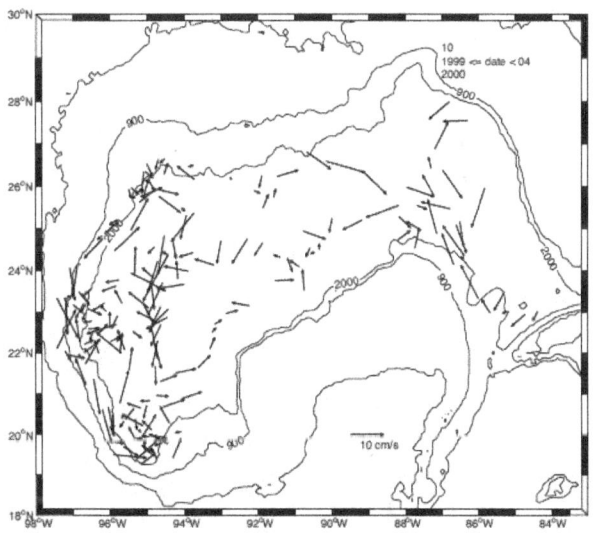

Fig. A4.

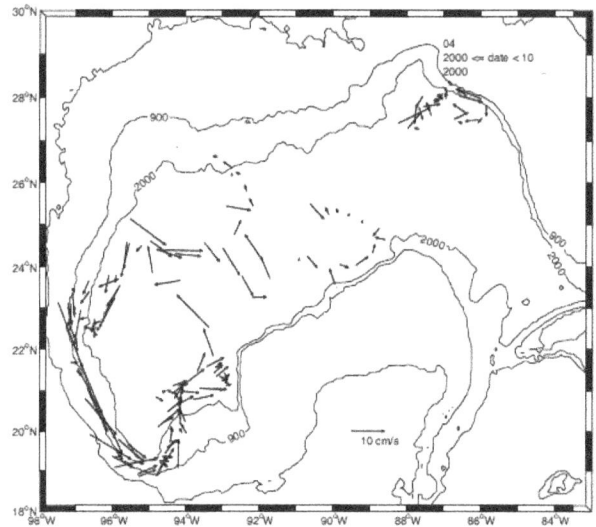

Fig. A5.

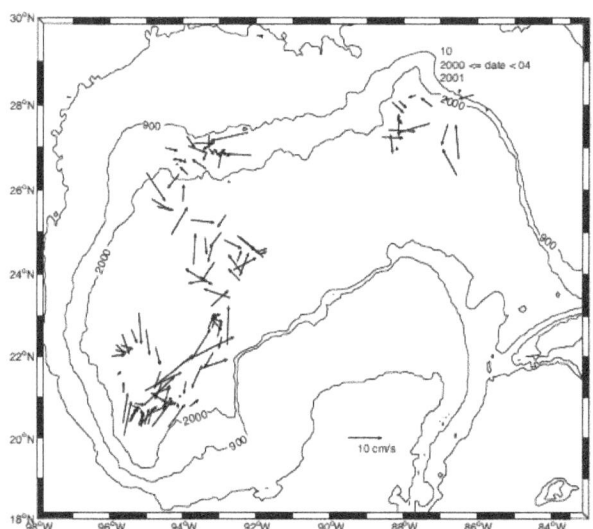

Fig. A6.

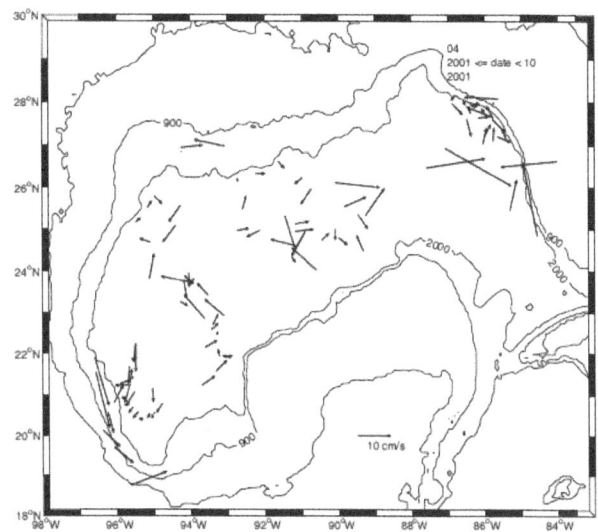

Fig. A7.

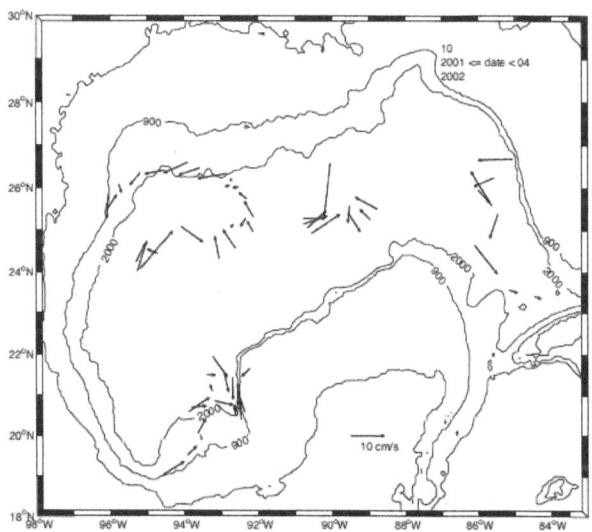

Fig. A8.

41

The Department of the Interior Mission

As the Nation's principal conservation agency, the Department of the Interior has responsibility for most of our nationally owned public lands and natural resources. This includes fostering sound use of our land and water resources; protecting our fish, wildlife, and biological diversity; preserving the environmental and cultural values of our national parks and historical places; and providing for the enjoyment of life through outdoor recreation. The Department assesses our energy and mineral resources and works to ensure that their development is in the best interests of all our people by encouraging stewardship and citizen participation in their care. The Department also has a major responsibility for American Indian reservation communities and for people who live in island territories under U.S. administration.

The Minerals Management Service Mission

As a bureau of the Department of the Interior, the Minerals Management Service's (MMS) primary responsibilities are to manage the mineral resources located on the Nation's Outer Continental Shelf (OCS), collect revenue from the Federal OCS and onshore Federal and Indian lands, and distribute those revenues.

Moreover, in working to meet its responsibilities, the **Offshore Minerals Management Program** administers the OCS competitive leasing program and oversees the safe and environmentally sound exploration and production of our Nation's offshore natural gas, oil and other mineral resources. The MMS **Minerals Revenue Management** meets its responsibilities by ensuring the efficient, timely and accurate collection and disbursement of revenue from mineral leasing and production due to Indian tribes and allottees, States and the U.S. Treasury.

The MMS strives to fulfill its responsibilities through the general guiding principles of: (1) being responsive to the public's concerns and interests by maintaining a dialogue with all potentially affected parties and (2) carrying out its programs with an emphasis on working to enhance the quality of life for all Americans by lending MMS assistance and expertise to economic development and environmental protection.